*RECLAIMING 1*

DISCARD

# RECLAIMING THE DREAM

*MARRIAGE COUNSELING IN THE PARISH CONTEXT*

## BRIAN W. GRANT

*ABINGDON PRESS*
*NASHVILLE*

RECLAIMING THE DREAM

Marriage Counseling in the Parish Context

*Copyright © 1986 by Abingdon Press*

This book is printed on acid-free paper.

**Library of Congress Cataloging-in-Publication Data**

GRANT, BRIAN W., 1939–
 Reclaiming the dream.
 1. Marriage counseling. 2. Pastoral counseling.
 3. Marriage—Religious aspects—Christianity. I. Title.
 BV4012.27.G73 1986 253.5 85-22841

**ISBN 0-687-35729-2 (pbk.: alk. paper)**

Scripture quotations are from the Revised Standard Version of the Bible, copyrighted 1946, 1952, © 1971, 1973 by the Division of Christian Education of the National Council of the Churches of Christ in the U.S.A. and used by permission.

MANUFACTURED BY THE PARTHENON PRESS AT
NASHVILLE, TENNESSEE, UNITED STATES OF AMERICA

# CONTENTS

*T*he occasion for this book was presented by a phone call in the fall of 1983 from my friend Paul Hopkins, requesting that I lead a workshop at the Samaritan Counseling Center in Amarillo, Texas. The lectures that formed the meat of that event have been expanded into the present work, along with the questions and comments of twenty-five pastors from the Texas Panhandle which entered into my thinking. I am grateful for the opportunity their invitation provided, and for the ongoing work they do.

Much of the thought content of this book has evolved from the past and present life of the Raines Pastoral Counseling Center in Indianapolis. It owes much to the stimulation of John Hinkle, Jackson Reed, Ed Alley, Linda Ferreria, Juanita Leonard, George Siskind, George Boyle, and Bob Kispert. Where their thought leaves off and my own begins is often hard to know.

A generation of students and clients of the center have also left their mark on this book. I especially thank John and Dee, Elliot and Sue, John and Ginger, Joe and Becky, and Bob and Charlene, who have taught me much about marriage by letting me know their marriages so well.

Thanks are due and offered at many levels to my wife, Claudia Ewing Grant, pastor of Central Christian Church in Lebanon, Indiana. She provides my ongoing rootage in the parish experience, and her 450 parishioners help keep me realistic about the pastoral task. She did a great deal of the actual work on this project: talking to publishers, negotiating contracts, providing editorial supervision, and telling me when I was and wasn't making sense. But most important, she has taught me what marriage can be, for which I'm profoundly grateful. She also has gone to more than her share of school music programs, doctors' offices, little league games, and Girl Scout outings because I've been writing. She may be the only person in the world who is happier than I am that it's finished. I thank her deeply.

Though this book is written primarily for pastors, seminarians, and students entering pastoral counseling and training programs in marriage and family therapy, there is no intent to be exclusive. Ninety-five percent of it is equally applicable to the work of professionals in a range of human service vocations, who occasionally are called on to work with troubled marriages. The techniques that help people love each other better are not the exclusive possession of any profession, and they are applicable across all such boundaries. My hope is that those who read further will be excited enough about the possibilities of being of use to couples in pain that they will make themselves available whenever possible, and with progressively developing skills.

# RECLAIMING THE DREAM

# CHAPTER ONE

# MARRIAGE:
# A DECISIVE ARENA
# FOR THE LOVE OF GOD

*M*any pressing needs compete for the pastor's time. The daily mail brings opportunities to upgrade a baffling array of skills. We can't possibly grow all the competence we need to serve the variety of people we encounter or to live up to our job descriptions, so we must develop our abilities in those areas we judge most important to our overall task and most fitted to our natural gifts.

Most clergy will not choose to become counseling specialists. They will see that function as a part of their overall calling and will judge that other tasks outweigh it, or that their own gifts are ill-suited to subtle, individualized, and time-intensive investment in alleviating psychic and relational pain. That is as it should be, and it assures the ongoing balance of repertoire that ministry as a profession requires to meet the breadth of its task.

But a fundamental understanding of the marital pain so rampant among our people, and the basic skills for assessing the structures that maintain and intensify that pain, are not optional. They are indispensable to basic professional competence and clerical faithfulness, even though the practitioner may never see a troubled couple for more than a session or two. Further, the mastery of a small number of straightforward interventions, building on those assessment skills, can make a significant difference in marital satisfaction for perhaps half the couples who seek you out, and can help you make competent and productive referrals for the others.

Failing to develop this minimal competence as part of the generalist practice of ministry, or of any other profession, leaves the practitioner unavailable as a resource in one of the most decisive areas of the congregation's life. A clear understanding, plus practiced competence in a small but well-thought-out repertoire of counseling tactics, can enable you to make a substantial contribution to the faithfulness of your people and the humanization of their community.

### God's Will Is for Human Love

"A new commandment I give to you, that you love one another; even as I have loved you, that you also love one another. By this all men will know that you are my disciples, if you have love for one another" (John 13:34-35).

Scripture and theology assert that human love is the strongest indicator of the presence and power of God. Throughout both Testaments the writers' attention regularly returns to the quality of relationships among the faithful, and between the faithful and the world. It is difficult to imagine a disciplined and devoted Christian community in which love for others is not a major and visible element.

Faithfulness itself is a product of love, both human and divine. We are most able to grow toward embodying the image of God when we live in loving relationships. Development of the peace and dignity that mark Christian maturity is much more difficult without relationships that encourage both parties to expose the self, to trust the other, and to expect good from the cosmos.

It is damaging to persons to live in an environment of chronic conflict. Self-protection then becomes more important than growth, loyalties develop in response to rivalry rather than cooperation, and opportunities for counterattack become more prized than chances to give. The converse is true when persons spend the bulk of their time in relationships that reward loving attitudes and behaviors. In these situations people learn that kindness is not always exploited, that revealing the truth about themselves often produces excitement and new knowledge, that making others feel better usually leads to their feeling better too. When one is the recipient of love, acting in a self-emptying, self-giving way is both safe and wise; and persons will experiment with becoming more Godlike in response to it.

John Calvin wrote that the chief end of humanity is to praise and enjoy God. People who experience love are those most likely to feel loving toward God and the world, and thereby those most likely to achieve that end. Situations wherein we feel loved and wish to return that love produce most of our raw gratefulness to God. It is then easier to praise, and far easier to enjoy. It could be said that no creation of God's is more central to the divine will than a human being who feels unconditionally loved and returns that love to all within reach, and beyond to God.

Human love has, indeed, a sacramental quality. It is a means of grace. None of us creates it in and of ourselves, but we receive it from those who love us and pass it on to those we love. It is, as Bernard Meland says of grace, "A good not our own."

A marriage relationship, moreover, is the central locus of that grace for many—perhaps most—people. The most fortunate among us had parents who created that kind of environment before we were born, and we had the opportunity, from earliest infancy, to breathe an atmosphere in which loving behavior was regularly modeled; in which we could concentrate on building a repertoire of responses, typically loving, to that stimulus. For those persons, the parental marriage is surely as sacramental as the Eucharist, and a part of what should be celebrated at every Thanksgiving.

For such fortunate youngsters, love has been learned through their parents' marriage. They have seen that it is possible for two adults to live in harmony and mutual enrichment, hence they know in principle that it is possible for them. Furthermore, they have seen how at least one couple does it, and they are most likely to model some aspects of the behavior of one or the other; and they have the luxury of being able to form their own personalities in a matrix rich with resources and relatively free of the relational dangers that lead people to protect themselves through constriction, anxiety, deception, and lowered expectations.

But most of us were not born into such unambiguously benign marriages. Our path into the knowledge of love is more difficult. If we make the best of our opportunities, we can arrive at adulthood somewhat equipped to share loving behavior with a spouse; hence marriage becomes the laboratory school in which we learn the complexities of love. We make various false starts as we attempt to fit our understandings with the understandings and preferences of the other. If we are fortunate, and if our longings for the satisfaction of closeness and our partner's happiness are stronger than our fear and anger about needing to change well-established patterns, our ability to love will grow. We will learn to create an environment in which it is safe and freeing to act lovingly. And we hope we will make major strides in that direction before our children are born so that they will enjoy the luxury of growing up in a richer milieu than did their parents.

Unfortunately, poised against that possibility of gradual increases in the level of lovingness from generation to generation, is the persistent transmission of obstacles to love, which also must be countered in every relationship. Every family also transmits its characteristic ways of closing off love, of pinching off the channels of transmission by the side effects of its methods of self-protection. Through anxiety, constriction, deception, covering, and attack, we strive to keep ourselves safe in the face of danger, but when these ways are overused they interfere with the self-giving and self-disclosure, the playfulness that love requires. They become the embodiment of sin.

That process takes place in two basic ways: We model our own self-protective devices on those used by our caretakers in childhood; and as we further develop those, we also fashion new devices to help us cope with the stress left by our parents' imperfection. Hence our parents' defenses affect us in two ways: by providing objects of imitation, from whom we learn how to protect ourselves; and by creating a situation of scarcity or danger in which we need to protect ourselves. When that protection exceeds the level needed to counter the actual danger, which it very often does, it becomes an obstacle to love.

That process operates even when environmental conditions are at their best, when the economy is booming, when society is stable or expanding, when community or family is available to provide a context for the individual, and when a sense of mastery and comfort with current technology holds sway. When any of those conditions is removed, a situation is created in which self-protection increases and the ease and naturalness of loving decrease. Persons who are coping fairly well three days out of four will often come apart at the seams if the economy takes a downturn, if their jobs are threatened, or if they have to move halfway across the country to a city where they have no friends. Their self-protectiveness and fear become worse yet if the jobs are lost, if industry is revolutionized by a new technology they don't understand, or if their extended families are fragmented by divorce, illness, or death. Their defensive maneuvers will increase, and along with them, the inner obstacles to love.

In any life, then, there is a constant tension between those forces that lead persons to disclose themselves to others, to give, to trust; and those that favor constriction, deception, and fear. When two lives join in marriage, this dynamic becomes more complex and volatile, in that each person now becomes a major part of comfort and/or stress for the other. How that blending works is crucial to what will be passed on to the next generation. When couples come to us for counseling, there usually has been a setback in the ability to keep loving and to transmit love-enhancing conditions to the children. The pastor is in a position to identify the factors that produce fear and hopelessness, and often can provide alternatives that will enable a couple to go back to learning more fully how to love, and how to teach that to others in their family. When that occurs, the balance between love and fear in the next generation has been improved, and the world has become more of a place where love is known and practiced. No objective that we seek is more valuable.

## Marriage and the Minister—
## Each Powerfully Affects the Other

In our society, the clergy have custody of marriage. Both because of the importance of marriage to the work of God, and because the society has designated ministers as the preferred performers of weddings, they have a special responsibility for the institution. And marriages, both their own and others', have a powerful impact on ministers.

There is no little irony in that. Marriage is a profoundly sexual arrangement, and clergy (especially male clergy) have long suffered from some suspicion about their sexual prowess and awareness. But it remains true that many people who would not want a clergyperson around for any other purpose, and who poke fun at clergy for their supposed sexual naiveté, want clergy to perform weddings and expect them to be experts on marriage itself. This appears when they present themselves for counseling.

Much of the influence clergy have on marriage is symbolic and liturgical, on the one hand, and emergency first aid on the other. But the same limited impact is not true of the effect of marriage on the clergy.

There is no factor in contemporary society, with the possible exception of secularism, that so disrupts the life of congregations as marital distress. As such it often deeply limits the effectiveness of churches to be the church and greatly complicates the pastors' fulfillment of professional responsibility.

To put it simply, when people are well married they are much more likely to be stable, settled, happy, and productive than when they are not. They are particularly more likely to have time and energy to invest in the church and other voluntary associations, because they are not needing to invest heavily in resolving a crucial, unresolved area of life. People whose romantic and sexual involvements are not satisfying usually make large investments in avoiding the pain in those relationships, trying to repair the damage or to develop new bonds with new people.

Since these activities take a lot of time, and since the church historically has been uncomfortable with people actively seeking new partners or in visible trouble with their old ones, it is time most often spent outside the church. The church isn't the only institution that suffers diminished investment when people's intimate relationships aren't working. Business involvements, volunteer activities, and same-sex friendships also are typically stressed, but rarely are those ties as specifically sensitive to sexual turbulence as is the church.

That complication becomes doubly painful for the congregation and the clergy when the marital upheaval leads to divorce. Divorces of couples active in the church almost always cost the congregation at least one participant. Even the one who "gets custody of the church" often does not have as much time, energy, and money to invest there, due to the high demands of single parenting, dual households, new dating relationships, and the fact that the couples-centered church does not have a ready place for newly single adults. So a congregation that had relied on a couple for two active and useful adult members will lose one completely and a half or a third of the other; and two adults who had had a stable life will enter a period of considerable pain and uncertainty. Marital problems deny the pastor the resources of an ally (or two) and add a major entry to the clerical list of problems.

The impact of marital problems on the clergy is not limited to the struggle they bring to the congregation. The stability and safety of the society as a whole is affected decisively by the quality of its marriages. In a recent sermon a minister recounted an incident in which a young couple he had married approached him about another matter. He gave them the assistance they requested, then asked them how the marriage was going. "Not so well," they said, "but that's our business." The minister challenged that statement immediately: "Everybody's marriage is my business." He went on to remind the couple that they would probably have children some day and that the happier and more stable their marriage, the less problem their children were likely to be to him and to everyone else. And so it is for all of us. Deep marital satisfaction on the part of one's parents is the best immunization against becoming a source of danger to the society. The children of marital pain lead the statistics in crime, child abuse, and divorce when they reach adulthood. Marital distress that a pastor can diminish makes the world safer for the pastor, and for the rest of us as well.

## Marriage and Human Growth

Clergy are inevitably involved in marriage, because of both their liturgical role and their theological commitments. And there are also substantial naturalistic and psychological reasons for their investment. For most persons, marriage is the most favorable context for growth. It is especially powerful as a tool for spiritual formation and for transmitting the results of that formation through the generations. As such, investments in marriage produce a huge return.

An intimate relationship with the same person over a long period of time—if that relationship is gratifying—is a revelation to us about the nature of the world and our own nature. It tells us, in a way that can't be doubted or disputed, that with the help of God and this other, we can establish a satisfying world and life. It tells us we can have companionship, challenge, conversation, sex, and fun. It tells us we can obtain help from another person when we need it. We are changed by knowing these things—self-esteem soars, fear shrinks, hope becomes natural and expectable. The goodness of creation feels like a reality, and gratitude is a spontaneous offering in return. The Gospel injunction, "Knock and it shall be opened to you," appears as a routine axiom for the management of life.

When people live in this situation, their need to protect themselves diminishes, leaving energy free for self-exploration, creativity, the attempt to express the self, and commitment to the core reality of other persons and of God.

Having established this satisfaction in a relationship, we usually find it worth our while to learn to deal with the problems that come to us because we are in relation to this particular other person. Through that dealing, we keep growing.

If you are married, stop and think for a minute about the information you have and the skills you have developed because you are married to your particular spouse. For most of us, the spouse comes equipped with loyalties, hobbies, physical problems and assets, friendships and families, all at least a little different from our own. Each spouse must develop a way of dealing with those particular facets of the partner. Someone told me recently that "because I'm married I've had the necessity and opportunity to learn about Judaism, the shoe business, diabetes, stepparenting, only children, Arkansas and Cleveland, plus my own snoring. I've also had to learn about jealousy, significant giving to the church, living with a pastor, raising children in a county seat, giving injections, and, most recently, horse racing."

Those discoveries are a mixture of pleasure and pain, but even the pleasant ones would probably have been missed had it not been for the choice to be with someone who considered it a matter of course that they would be in Cleveland every so often, or that the shoe business is as basic to life as eating and has a culture all its own.

But even more important are the discoveries that haven't been so pleasant. Living with a chronic and potentially life-shortening disease is not something most of us would choose, but choosing a spouse who has such a disease teaches a person some valuable things there are no other ways to learn. The same is true of all the differentnesses of spouses. Whether it's their ordinal position in the family, or the particular way their family is close and/or fragmented, or whether they like to read in bed at night, that reality presents something inescapable that must be dealt with.

That's decisively different from what happens with those realities we decide to master for other reasons. Many new experiences in life we choose for pleasure, pursue further if they remain pleasurable, and quit when they stop being fun. That's why most adults no longer play a musical instrument, take ballet, or spend their spare time working algebra problems. So when we meet people different enough to make us grow, but who don't offer the promise of the type and magnitude of gratification necessary for us to consider marrying them, the very fact of their differentness will persuade us to leave them out of our intimate lives.

The satisfaction promised by the person-who-will-be-spouse is the lure that pulls us into the new learning. That, in turn, expands our being and continues to refine us as persons, as we combine the newness with what we already have inside. Some would see this lure of love as being precisely the work of God.

An additional marital factor in spiritual growth is the ongoing lifelong supervision by someone with a life and death stake in our overall health, and in our seeing the truth about ourselves. Like some of the problems our choice of spouse brings us, this gift is not always welcome; but if lovingly and skillfully practiced, it functions like a disciplined spiritual direction, gradually addressing itself to each of the areas in which we defeat our own growth—with the exception of those areas where we and our spouse share a blind spot. Everything is vulnerable to feedback in marriage: the way we drive, the clothes we wear, the extent to which we take care of ourselves physically and emotionally, our parenting skills, our lovemaking, the way we practice ministry.

The crucial difference between this feedback and that which one gets from others is that this person's whole future counts on every comment. He or she can't afford not to be heard if the matter is really important, which makes the input more impassioned and the transaction more complicated. Hence she or he will often risk saying things that others, more dependent on one's approval or less willing to risk for one's welfare, will avoid. The hardest things for the spouse to say are typically those one most needs to hear and those least likely to come from anyone else.

This particular element of marital interaction is particularly sensitive to the overall quality of the relationship and the trust between the spouses; hence it is an element that counseling influences strongly. When spouses are more frightened and angry toward each other than loving, this supervision becomes a weapon that can destroy. A man said to me once that every time he became a little less depressed, his wife found something new to attack him with. What he saw as attacks, she saw as bringing up important issues for them to face together, but his momentary lack of trust deprived him of this resource. In a close marriage, spouses know it is in their interest to hear the feedback, and the spouse becomes a stand-in for the Spirit, from whom there is no place to flee.

## The Current History of Marriage

The current position of marriage in its own historical development makes the role of the pastor as marriage counselor particularly important now. Though it is probably true that all times are difficult in their own way, since the late 1950s there have been huge shifts in the way the majority of marriages in this country are conducted, in what people have wanted out of those marriages, in the skills that have been needed to reach those goals, and in the broader societal context in which those marriages have been embedded. The shifts have left immense segments of the population needing more from marriage because many of their other supports have been removed, but without the necessary skills for getting what they need. In such times people in a position to teach the needed skills are a vital cultural resource.

From the time of the Neolithic revolution, when women reportedly discovered agriculture and men discovered that it was pleasant to have regular meals and a consistent roof over their heads, settled communities became much more prevalent. Marriage, and possibly monogamy, became an option. At this point the family was primarily a productive unit. Men and women worked to produce agricultural goods and the support services and implements that provided the basis for those efforts. The more children they had, the more help there was with the work, the more product was possible, and the greater their chances for survival as a family. Sexual function within the marriage primarily served reproduction, and reproduction—along with the whole marital cycle—was primarily a matter of survival.

In this structure, marriage and family were very broad relationships. They had to provide practically everything for their members: education, religious instruction, sexual satisfaction, production of goods, services, and income, medical care, and all other necessities.

During those times people selected mates for different reasons than they do now. It was a matter of survival that a mate be hardy, in good health, a good worker, skilled at a range of domestic and mechanical duties, and reliable, in order to provide the basics of the physical and psychological environment in which a person could grow. Marital choice in such a society was a thoroughly practical matter. People with given skills needed spouses with complementary skills; and emphasis on the spouse's relationship ability or sexual attractiveness was much less.

The industrial revolution brought a further immense change, at least to the urban marriage, as first men, then women and children moved more and more from the family farm, shop, or business and into a factory or other place of work. That broke one form of traditional marriage and led to women's work becoming more specific and homebound for many generations. Urbanization accompanied this change, and specialized religious and educational institutions took over primary functions in those areas. As the money economy became more prevalent, services that previously were obtained primarily from one's spouse, parent, or child became more and more purchasable outside the home. Hence it became less important that one's spouse could make soap. One could buy it. As this change progressed, people became less dependent upon what they could manufacture for themselves, so less of the weight of relationships could be sustained by one's spouse being a good provider, a good cook, seamstress, or whatever.

Hence modern marriage has become a vastly more specialized relationship than ever before. The modern battle for survival is more an emotional battle than a physical one, and the modern function of marriage has become more the mutual fulfillment of emotional needs than a striving for economic productivity. So the reasons for marital choice are properly different than they were a few generations ago, and the conditions for the continuation of a marriage have also changed.

This change has come about so rapidly that most of us find ourselves living in marriages that are styled according to this newer model, with the primary goals being companionship and mutual personal growth; but we grew up in families headed by parents whose marriage was structured and contracted according to a more traditional model. Because of that, many of us are having to learn the basic skills of intimacy for the first time in our marriages, having been raised in families where intimacy was a secondary goal, lower in priority than the performance of various physical survival skills.

That transition has created very serious dilemmas. Many couples who come for counseling say that both spouses are so unskilled in the whole range of intimate behavior that their marriage is not a source of strength and satisfaction. Others come with one person having discovered his or her own potential for intimacy in experiences other than marriage and feeling angry and cheated that the spouse has not made a similar discovery.

Part of the pain of this situation is a result of our increasingly mobile society—more and more, it's true that one's spouse is the only person available with whom to share a long-term deeply personal relationship. There was a time when people grew up in a neighborhood with a group of friends and relatives, went to school, took a job there, got married, continued most of their lives in that neighborhood, and were buried from the corner mortuary. In that era, a man might spend many of his companionship-seeking hours at the community bar with the fellows he graduated from high school with, the men he worked with at the plant, and be able to escape loneliness even if his marriage were a wasteland. A woman was likely to have the same neighbors at forty that she had at fourteen, as well as the support of extended family. But with our increasing mobility, these relationships are perpetually interrupted. The guys at the corner bar are strangers; and more often than not, mothers or sisters are a thousand miles away. When you combine that with the greater specialization of the marriage relationship, it's obvious that the person whose marriage is not satisfying is often trapped in a very lonely world. Nothing else the spouses can do for each other is now irreplaceable; my wife can always call a plumber. But if there is no one else within five miles of home whom I've known for more than two years, my relationship with her becomes a matter of psychological life and death.

So the reasons for the high divorce rate cannot be reduced to the inability of people to live together, but must include the radically heightened goals and expectations for the emotional relationship between spouses. There once was a time when it wasn't too important if a spouse made you feel more alive when you met at the apartment door in the evening, as long as the meal was cooked and the laundry done; but now I can hire the cooking and laundry done. But there may not be anyone else in my world who cares whether I'm alive or not.

So if a person begins to doubt that the spouse really does care, or that his or her caring is about the same things in me that I care about, divorce with its attendant dislocation and cost is an understandable option. It's happening so often not because people don't want marriage, but because they are longing for something they expect to find in marriage. The problem, very often, is that they don't know how to get it; and almost as often, they do not have the inner resources either to get it or to give what it costs—so knowing how is not enough.

This is the situation in which we practice marital counseling. People want very much to be married, and to get from marriage what they see as obtainable only there. But they see a lot of failure around them, and they are skeptical and frightened that it may not be possible to have what they believe they need. In that fear, they often pull back into self-protection, making it even less likely they can get it.

When we bring hope into such a situation, we are faithful to our calling.

# *P*ASTORAL
# *BEGINNINGS FOR*
# *MARRIAGE COUNSELING*

*T*he logical question now is, How do we begin? The answer is, You have already begun.

If you are a pastor, or any publicly recognized leader of a religious community, the first steps of marriage counseling have begun in the existing interactions with the people you serve—in the perceptions they have of you, your marriage, your views about marriage in general, and their marriage in particular.

## The Process Begins Before They Call

The research on healing is unanimous on one point: The expectation of being helped is the most powerful factor in whether an intervention is helpful. Because that is true (see Jerome Frank, *Persuasion and Healing,* Johns Hopkins, 1961), the process of receiving help has been underway from the first time a prospective counselee was aware of you. As people have seen you work, heard what you say, and been aware of the public face of your private life, they have been deciding whether you are a person they would expect to be helpful, should they get into marital difficulties. You have already begun their healing: by embodying, teaching, and preaching a view of marriage.

One thing makes you different from office therapists—you have direct influence, through your public statements, over a part of their selection process. Your preaching will either directly or indirectly convey what you think about marriage in general, much as the first chapter of this book conveys my thoughts on the subject. People who find those thoughts compatible with their own hopes and dreams for their relationship are much more likely to come to you for help than are those who object to what you say.

In addition to your ideology, about which you speak from time to time, they will also be listening for the indirect communications you offer in sermons. They will be alert to the view of marriage that comes through in illustrations intended for other subjects. They will catch the tone of voice in which you refer to the marriages of people you're preaching about. They will be affected by your choice of texts that convey particular attitudes about relations between the sexes, even if that wasn't the point you were trying to make. In other words, if they are beginning to sense marriage as a point in their lives that may need some attention, they're going to be scanning the environment, at least unconsciously, for signs that the potential helping people either are or are not the ones they will seek. Those who like what they hear are much more likely to seek you out; and their expectation that you will be helpful is an important part of the resources they bring to the counseling.

Interestingly, some people will seek you out because they *don't* like what you say. Often you won't discover this until the process is finished, but they will either have been looking for a counselor they don't agree with so they don't have to take the process seriously; or, in more fortunate instances, have sensed something in the viewpoint or attitude you represent that they know they must come to grips with, perhaps because the spouse shares it.

There are other ways, besides your public statements, in which you begin marital counseling before the first appointment. Not only do you speak to the community you share with prospective counselees, you also live in it. Its members will know a lot about some aspects of your marriage and will have formed judgments about how accurately it reflects what you say about marriage in public. If they sense agreement between what you say and what they see, they are more likely to identify you as a potential help giver. Your trustworthiness will have been enhanced.

They will know whether you have chosen a spouse they like; and they will make some judgment about whether the criteria you apparently used in that selection fit the ideology you preach and the ideals they have. They will know whether you and your spouse publicly enjoy each other, whether you talk to each other in public on a more or less equal plane; they will know if you are about as likely as your spouse to show up at the Little League game, family night at the school, the high school music contest, or the emergency room when it's your kid who's been hit by a pitch. They will certainly have noticed such obvious details as whether your spouse works and what kind of job it is—not to mention whether your job seems to be prioritized ahead of your spouse's, behind, or equal. They will know something about whether you take time off, and how you spend at least some of it. Hence they will know whether you share public leisure activities, and they will have some idea about the quantity of them you take in. And they will know the extent to which your spouse is involved in your professional life, and you in his or hers. They will have noticed whether your spouse goes with you to make speeches, to call on shut-ins, to attend conventions. They will know to what extent he or she is involved in the church, and whether that seems to be because it is enjoyed, or because it is either the thing to do or you seem to demand it.

While they are noticing all these things, they are getting an impression of what they can expect from you as a marriage counselor. It's important for you to know how your congregation's particular set of perceptions and expectations is being formed and what it consists of. If it's not what you would have it be, it may require some intentional work on your part.

Almost always, people will let you know in the first few minutes of a counseling process what they expect and why they have come to expect it. If they don't do it directly, and there's any ambiguity about it whatever, it's important to ask. If the reply is not what you would hope for, you may have some changes to make.

## How and Why People Come

Most couples who marry have a dream, a hope that their relationship will do the things for them that fit their image of fulfillment. They come for marital counseling when their hope in the dream is slipping away, when they fear they will lose it unless they do something out of the ordinary, or when the cost of maintaining the dream seems too high.

### Indirect Beginnings and a Pastoral Response

The first contacts for marriage counseling in the parish are often indirect, hurried, and in code. People often see you in public situations, where they have a chance to exchange only a sentence or two before someone comes up and joins the conversation. Communication in those situations is more often hinted at than fully declared, and it's typically up to the pastor to pursue the full meaning.

The opening words of a counseling relationship are often mumbled at the church door after services or in the kitchen during fellowship. "I've been meaning to stop by the office" or "There's something I've wanted to talk to you about" are often about as much as can be said before the next parishioner is within earshot or it's time to return to the business. The next few exchanges are crucial to whether any help is actually conveyed. Often there is so little time that only a meaningful glance or possibly a word—"Please give me a call" or "I'll be in the office in the morning"—can be offered to convey that you really do want the contact to continue, but not so eagerly that the other is taken aback. Further, if anyone else can hear, your response must be disguised enough that it could be understood as a routine business remark. If it's clear you won't be overheard, it must convey a touch of knowing that something of emotional importance is about to be unveiled.

If the phone does ring the next morning, or the person comes round to the office, then your task is relatively simple. Either the person says, "I've wanted to talk to you about my marriage," or after a long pause you say, "There was something you wanted to see me about." But often the parishioner does not make it that easy for you. There is no call or visit for two or three days. It would be easy to forget, but a deacon mentions having seen the woman in the grocery store and noticed that she seemed awfully depressed. Sometimes your past experience with this person will tell you how long to wait, knowing that some people will regard a day's delay as indifference and others will see a call two weeks later as presumptuous meddling.

But more often, you will need to take responsibility for that decision without a lot of data to guide you. One factor to be considered is time—when will you actually have time to talk, possibly at length. When you do, and within a few days of the initial remark, I'd suggest a phone call that asks, rather neutrally, whether the other would like to follow up on what was mentioned after church or at the meeting the other day. If the answer is no, or not right now, or call me back tonight (someone may be listening at the other end), it's imperative to follow the person's lead with "I'll be thinking about you" or "When it's time, let me know," and tag the file in your mind as one that may come up again soon.

But if the answer is yes, then a counseling relationship has probably begun, and the next words need to be said with that in mind. There's less chance of getting off on the wrong foot if you find out right away the kind of concern the parishioner intends to bring. You will know more about how much time to allot and be in a better position to suggest whether the person should come alone or invite other people who may be involved in the issue. "Can you tell me enough over the phone to give me an idea what's involved?" will often elicit clues. Of course, some people may prefer to say nothing until they are in your presence, and that needs to be honored; but if the reply is "Well, it's about our marriage" or "I need some help with my wife," then you have important information.

That little bit makes a difference because it enables you to say "Do you think she'd come in with you?" or "Have you talked with him about this?" Obviously, this can be tricky and needs to be handled delicately, but nonetheless you are in a much better position to begin an intervention in a marriage if you have access to both parties from the beginning. People who have not been part of the process at the start often become frightened or angry about what their spouse may have said in their absence, or what you may have agreed with them about. That's not an insuperable barrier, and I never refuse to see one spouse alone without strong reason. But while you are in a position to influence whether you are able to begin with both together, it's best to take advantage of it to make your job easier.

Often people who start their quest for help with the pastor don't believe in the value of open communication about marital conflict. You may run into horrified negatives about the idea of having the spouse come in. If that happens, it's best to accept that those people will have trouble extending such an invitation, and that you'll have to talk about attempting it once you have them in the office with you. If you do find it necessary to accept that arrangement, it will be helpful to let them know it isn't a closed issue forever. A comment like, "Well, let's talk about that when you're here. I can see you Thursday morning at 9:00," is in order. When Thursday morning rolls around, though, it does need to be dealt with.

Another situation for the pastor differs from that of the office therapist—sometimes it's not the potential counselee who lets you know about the trouble. Pastors often hear from third parties about difficulties in a parishioner's marriage.

"Marge just told me that John and Mary have separated."

"I'm the guidance counselor at the school, and little Jamie is in here crying about the fight his parents had this morning. He said maybe you could help."

"Joan was just in here in a fury. She says Bill beat her up last night, and she has the bruises to prove it."

These are not messages the pastor is glad to receive, both because of the pain they report and because they ask for one of the most difficult interventions pastors ever are called on to make. But once you have the information, you're stuck with it and have to make a decision to do either something or nothing. Only if the informant is notably unreliable is it best to disregard the message. Even then some discreet inquiries, without revealing the source of your curiosity, would be in order. To say to an elder that you haven't seen John and Mary for a couple of months gives him or her a chance to tell you anything they know about the situation, without your having to compromise confidentiality. If the report won't go away, if no other information tells you to ignore it, then eventually a contact is in order—and more often sooner than later.

Knowing what to say is not the hardest part of this situation; the hardest part is dealing with the feelings about saying it. The message is simple: "Someone has told me you're in pain. I know you haven't invited me, but I'm concerned and available if you want anything from me."

Sometimes people are relieved to have you discover their problem, and sometimes they are angry and embarrassed that you found out at all. But the anger at you is usually short-lived, and if a rift ensues it was already in the making. The rift usually occurs because the parishioners have done things that place them at odds with the church or people who are part of the church, and not specifically because you found out and said something to them. The pastor's fear is of being accused of meddling in something where you have no business, but you have business everywhere your people's welfare is at stake. They can relieve you immediately of any responsibility to take an active part, but you can't decide responsibly, in advance of speaking to them, that their pain has no claim on you.

In either situation—that of the spouse who has let you know indirectly of a problem, or the crisis that comes to your attention through a third party—the important step is to elicit from those concerned a clear statement of needing and wanting your involvement, or of neither needing nor wanting it. With a positive statement, counseling can begin, and it can be clear to everyone that you are involved because they want something you have to offer, rather than that you are meddling in their lives.

## The First Hour in Your Office

Once both spouses or, if unavoidable, only one of them, are actually in your office, the first task is to find out exactly what is troubling them. After a brief exchange of pleasantries, if a short pause doesn't bring out a description of their problem, a gentle inquiry into the cause and purpose of the visit will usually get things started. Something like, "Can you tell me why you've come and what you hope I can help you change?" is my preference. It puts the responsibility on them, indicates that you want to help but it is they who will do the changing, and is open-ended enough that they will often provide quite a bit of information.

Out of that often jumbled mass of fact and feeling, it is indispensable to obtain some data very precisely. You must find out, preferably in the first half hour, exactly what the problem is. You need to know the problem from both sides, if both spouses are available, since eventually you will need a jointly agreeable statement of it. Often people will try to gloss it over with generalizations that make it impossible to understand or that make it sound much more or less serious than it is. Statements like "We just can't communicate" or "We're fighting all the time" are a beginning but only that. It is necessary to pursue the inquiry until you know just what they need to communicate but aren't saying; whether it's a matter of not saying the things they need to say, or more of both believing the other doesn't hear them when they speak; or whether there are just certain subjects they aren't communicating on, or that they can't even say "Pass the salt" and get the salt. Sometimes people use that introduction when the problem is that they're communicating all too well; the fact being that they don't like each other, or don't like what the other is communicating.

There's a series of questions I need the answers to before I believe I understand the problem: How often? To what extent? Under what conditions? When who's around? With what consequences? What happens next? By the time this section of the first interview is over the counselor needs to be able to describe the cross section of the problem that the couple most wants help with. The description should include how the troubling interaction starts, when it's most likely to come up, whose presence makes it more or less likely (some couples won't fight at all if the kids are there, but will every time her mother comes), what seems to be at stake when it happens, how they've been able to stop it in the past, what usually happens when it's over, how long it's likely to be before it happens again, and what it will take to initiate the next cycle. You also need to know what emotions people on both sides of the conflict are typically feeling at each stage, and how severe a threat to the relationship they judge it to be. That's another way of asking "How much time do we have to solve this before it reaches the point of no return?"

Another important variable is needed in the first session— why did they come for help right now? Often they will tell you this same thing has been happening for years (always find out how long it's been going on), but they only decided to call this week because it got .05 percent worse. You can get a broader picture when they tell you what brought their problem to the place where they had to let somebody else know about it; this lets you know where the threshold is for believing the dream is in jeopardy. Often people put up with stuff from spouses that nobody else in the world would tolerate, but decide it can't go any further when somebody forgets to water the prize rose bush, or lets some neighbor hear a tone of voice that previously had been reserved for private discussion, or strings out an argument so that one spouse is late for a golf game. Hearing what that breaking point is lets you know the current danger level, and also tells you something about the priorities within the original dream.

This part of the interview is finished when you can make a detailed statement of the nature of the problem, get the agreement of both parties to that statement, and believe yourself that this problem is causing as much distress as they say it is.

The agreement can usually be achieved by a careful rewording of the description of the problem. Typically, the spouse who talks first will describe the problem in terms that the other would not or does not like. "She's always yelling at me" is one side of a description of a complex process, usually including a provocative act or statement or inaction on *his* part. "He never comes home on time" similarly picks up the piece of a problematic sequence that is most troubling to one spouse, but ignores the question of *her* part of the problem. An important part of the counselor's skill. is to keep the conversation alive until you get enough pieces to enable a mutually acceptable definition of the problem.

"You haven't been able to agree on how much time to spend together and how to make that time enjoyable enough so that you both want it," is an example of a mutually acceptable definition. That should be followed with supporting descriptions: "You feel he should be home more, and you'd be willing to be home more if you weren't so certain she'd be attacking you for not having been home yesterday; you say you'd want to be home more if you could get back to the way things were between you before the baby was born . . . ." In the example of "She's always yelling at me," the mutually acceptable definition might be: "You've never settled the question of who's going to take responsibility for which tasks around the house, and when you, Mary, see one you think he should be doing and it isn't done, you explode; but you, John, contend that it's never been settled that that's your job. Maybe my task is to help you negotiate over who is going to do what."

Often the first time or two you rephrase the problem, you won't get it quite right. Someone will insist that one of the words is wrong, or you've left something out that's important. Keep at it until you get it right for both of them, adding and modifying terms until it seems to suit them each about equally. Once you have settled on a description, you have made a major step toward a counseling contract. It only remains for you to say that this problem is one you can help them with, and for them to say that's the help they want. If you accept a statement of the problem that favors the concerns of one more than those of the other, you've agreed to help change what is painful for one but not for the other. That isn't fair, the person who is less well served will know it, and that person's cooperation will not be available to get the job done. An even-handed contract is indispensable if you are to do valuable work that has the endorsement of both partners. It's worth the time and attention to detail to get it right.

Drawing up such a statement is doubly difficult when only one spouse has come for the first interview; this is why it is so important to have both involved as early as possible. (A major exception is made when one spouse has significant doubts about whether to put any more effort into the marriage—usually when a third party is involved. In that situation it will usually be necessary to see that spouse alone until such time as he or she has decided whether to make an investment in the relationship.) If the individual work has not prejudiced the counselor in favor of one partner, and if the other spouse trusts the work, then you can go ahead and see them both. In other situations, where favoritism or distrust is marked, referral to another counselor is necessary.

When only one spouse is seen, the process of the first session is the same, with the addition of a central question about why it was impossible to involve the other spouse. If the other spouse was not invited, I always want to know why, and I am usually suspicious of the answers. Sometimes it's self-evident—perhaps the spouse in your office wants to decide what to do about an affair the partner is not aware of; but more often the expressed reason will itself be a signal of something that needs treating. You will sense either the fear of the partner you are seeing: "He'd kill me if he knew I was telling you this"; or the wish to prejudice you before the other partner has a shot: "I just wanted you to know how things really are before we see you together."

When the partner you're with expresses fear, you have to make an assessment of that judgment. If the fear is of actual violence, I always ask if the spouse has been violent before and, if not, why this situation is different. Sometimes there does seem to be a reason, but more often the fear diminishes in the face of questioning. If the spouse has been violent before, it usually has been in a more impulsive situation, often when drinking was involved, and careful strategizing about ways to structure the situation can diminish the threat. Obviously there are situations in which the danger is real and must be taken seriously. If the counseling appears to increase rather than decrease the danger, people will not come, and should not. Then individual counseling aimed at preparing the wife to ask the husband in an effective way, or targeted on helping her to free herself from either the relationship itself or its fearsomeness, is in order.

Most of the time, however, the reluctance is not a result of such dramatic and dangerous possibilities. It typically relates more to the desire of the one who has sought you out to place the other in the wrong, or simply to ignorance of the marital counseling process. Often you can role-play effective ways of asking the other spouse to come and help develop an effective method. Or if counselees have already asked a spouse, done it badly, and been refused, it is possible to go back through the way it was done, find the inflammatory or indecisive phrases, and coach them on how to start over, undo the damage, and issue an invitation that will be persuasive. Clients have the best chance of securing a spouse's participation if they speak directly; if they emphasize that you are an objective third party, rather than someone who will represent the client's point of view exclusively; and if they dispassionately but firmly point out the dangers to the relationship, and to the other spouse's comfort, if the problems are not worked out.

If after extended conversation, clients simply can't get it right or they've made attempts that have misfired, the counselor may make the invitation directly. Because of the tightness of your schedule and the need of spouses to learn to talk directly to their partners, it's better if they can do it themselves. But after a failure or two, or if there is compelling reason it is not feasible, a call from you, indicating that you have seen the spouse, that you have a picture of the problems from that perspective and would like to get a more balanced view before proceeding, will usually bring the other in at least once. Once reluctant spouses have entered the office, and you get a chance to demonstrate your competence and ability to make the situation safe, they very often will agree to continue.

### *The Early Information and What It Means*

What people tell you in the first hour almost always lets you know whether you're dealing with a dream in serious danger or one in need of only a modest adjustment, and will usually give you a good idea of the cost to the couple of maintaining their dream, improving it, or leaving it as it is or was.

If it is a workable dream but is beginning to wander off the path and needs a bit of mid-course correction, it usually displays specific signs. To begin with, there have been some good times, some times when the dream seemed workable and the progress toward it seemed solid. Furthermore, though there may be a lot of current anger, and the disagreements about what is happening now can be quite heated, there won't be the derisiveness that leaves you thinking each would just as soon the other be dead. There will be the ability to remember the good times—they won't be terribly long ago—and they usually will be able to tell you that if this or that disagreement is worked out, they could see themselves back on the path toward achieving what they'd always wanted.

But the present disagreements can be pretty intense, even at this level, and a couple's fear that they won't settle them can be very strong. In this category of problem, a signal that something has gone off the track in the relationship can show up in one spouse having an affair, or in some other outside involvement, not necessarily sexual, which becomes important enough to be scary to one or both parties. In this level of difficulty fights occur over one spouse not staying home enough or the two of them not getting enough time together, suggesting that something new is producing distance between them. This level of marital difficulty is the same as that expressed when a youngster acts up in a not-too-dangerous way—for instance, when one who has been a B student begins to get Cs and an occasional D, or gets into the kind of conflict with teachers that results in being kept after school two or three times in a month. But if a child suddenly begins to flunk everything, something worse is happening. Obviously, this is also true if a previously model child begins to stay out all night and then is expelled for carrying a concealed weapon. Brief episodes of alcohol or drug abuse in married persons never in trouble before also signal a marital struggle that needs treatment but is probably readily manageable. The same is true of newly emerging fights over whether one or the other is watching too much television, going to church too often, or becoming overinvolved in work.

This is often the level of problem that can be resolved promptly by focusing on communication skills, so that people can negotiate with new confidence and thus settle problems that grew up in the absence of those skills. We'll talk more about those methods in Chapters 4 and 5. In terms of individual pathology, these are usually people with low-level, garden-variety neuroses or adjustment problems, who would never seek treatment for individual difficulty. But when their marital dreams begin to decay and they see the danger of losing what they dreamed marriage was to achieve for them, they will really exert an effort to try to get what they feel they must have. In struggling to raise the temperature of the relationship and of their lives, they will often make a fairly dramatic and painful, if short-lived, mess. People with this level of pain will almost never create disasters, but they will get into difficulties through misguided or poorly resourced attempts to increase the emotional yield they receive from walking their paths together.

The next group of people, those who come to see a counselor because the costs of pursuing their dream are becoming too great, are more capable of creating disasters. They will come complaining of more florid crises, and their manner in the session will be more intense. This group can be divided into two major types, and each requires a very different kind of intervention: those in situational crises that demand prompt stabilization, and those in which individual pathology has chosen the marriage as an arena for acting out.

The situational problems are much easier to deal with, but have the disadvantage of urgency: If something isn't done promptly, damage will result. The classic precipitants of these crises occur at the family boundaries: Someone enters or leaves the family, or something stops or changes. Death is a paradigm for these crises: The whole family must change—members must assume new roles, deal with their grief, handle the changed economic and emotional situation while continuing to carry on in the external world. The arrival of stepchildren in a blended family is another classic, since the whole role structure in a previously settled relationship network has to change. Serious physical illness or emotional difficulties also fit into this category; both effectively remove family members from their normal functions for a time and threaten to make them permanently unavailable in a way that frightens and stresses everyone. Financial crises stemming from job loss or layoff throw families into a similar crunch (these people are especially likely to seek pastoral help because it's often free), and require major resetting of tasks and expectations. A family move or a major improvement in financial position will similarly throw things out of kilter and mean that gratifications once available no longer are and that some stressors that didn't exist in the former situation have become commonplace.

Timeliness is the critical variable in these situations. The interventions are not difficult, but if they don't happen soon enough, things can get away from the people involved, and more desperate and perhaps dangerous solutions will be tried. Often, setting an appointment to talk about the pain is the decisive step. All such crises create extra work for all the members of a family, and in the crush they often haven't found time to talk face to face about the changes, how to adjust to them, how to keep anyone from receiving more than a fair share of the pain or the glory. Misunderstandings and feelings of persecution grow up easily in these circumstances, and people often feel it's against the rules to say anything about their feelings. All this is reinforced by the fact that everyone is under stress from the changes, which often makes the anger level high and the trust level low—all of which interferes mightily with reflective conversations.

The counselor's role in that situation often boils down to providing the time, the place, and the safety for the conversations. The pastor can help the couple discover that Susie's newly noticed sulking happens every time mom is talking with her new friend, which gives mom a chance to say and do some reassuring things with Susie; you can help them recognize that dad is gone about ten hours a week more now than before the move, and he can let mom and the kids know the details of his new responsibilities and how long the crunch will last. You can help them find a way to talk about the fact that the newly transplanted stepchild really misses her old family but has been afraid to talk about it for fear of reprisals; and you can help her new family find ways of saying they do want to be liked and that they understand the reality of the child's feelings.

These situational crisis interventions are often very satisfying, with the counselor providing the lubrication for the moves the family half-knew it needed to make anyway. If something isn't done, there is high risk; but it's hard to mess it up if you keep the conversation flowing and make sure everyone's interests are spoken to.

The final category is more difficult, and of a type a pastor will often want to refer elsewhere. Some people experience the cost of trying to pursue their dream, at least with their present partner, as exorbitant on an ongoing basis. The events that are costly will be reported as occurring over a long period of time, and their severity will be obvious, once they are mentioned. These are the couples whose poor impulse control shows up in chronic financial difficulties, more with overspending than with underearning; or in recurring cycles of violence against spouse or children. These are the couples in which one or both spouses struggle or have struggled with long-term alcohol or substance abuse, often having found each other when one or both were drinking. These are the couples whose children are the terror of the neighborhood, acting up in the same way for years, failing in school, involved in violence or long-term promiscuity.

In such cases, you can see at a glance that it has been very costly to both spouses to be with each other for years. Any intervention that will make a significant difference would have to enhance the personal development of both of them in a major way. Typically these are people who can make life quite difficult for someone who tries to help them, and this difficulty is doubly complicated when you have a public role that involves dealing with them on a regular basis. These involvements require all the training and time that normally go with the title psychotherapist, and unless the pastor wishes to make such a major investment of self, these people had best be referred as soon as possible. They are difficult for the most experienced of therapists, and good stewardship of the pastor's time suggests that his or her life and work will run more smoothly and productively if someone else is their counselor.

# CHAPTER THREE

# *COURTSHIP HAPPENS IN A DEVELOPMENTAL CONTEXT*

*T*o be valuable to couples beyond the first hour, and often to make the second twenty minutes useful, we need to know how marriages in general develop and how the marriage we have in front of us has grown. If we have developed an overview of the role marriages play in the lives of persons and communities, we also have a road map for our reconnaisance of this particular marriage. The next two chapters will lay out a theory of marital selection, explain what that choice means in the personal development of each partner, and present a plan for getting the information a counselor needs to understand the development of any individual marriage.

## We Want Different Things at Different Ages

Young men and women begin learning to court one another almost as soon as they are aware of sexual differences, and they continue until they are firmly committed to a partner. But the way people conduct courtship changes as time passes. We court differently at different ages, since we have learned new skills; and we need different things from our partners as we grow older, since we usually have developed more of our own capacities and have less need to choose partners who will fill a gap in ourselves. Further, what we have to offer changes, since we have developed skills and gifts that alter (we hope, increase) our actual usefulness to a potential mate.

Therefore as time passes, we rank differently in the potential competition for members of the opposite sex. Some of our attributes become less important, and things we are newly learning take on higher value. As we move from age 14 to 18, our willingness to oppose parental authority usually counts for less, and our ability to drive a car becomes more of an asset. As we move from 18 to 22, it comes to matter less for most of us whether we are picked as cheerleader or hit the jump shot, and it becomes more important that we win a degree or hold a faith. And as we move from 22 to 35, our raw physical attractiveness is likely to become less important, and our ability to hold a meaningful conversation about a topic of vital interest becomes more so.

Because these things are true, marriages that are contracted on a first date at age 14 are different from those contracted at 30. Couples that get together in their first year of high school and stay together four years till marriage, are usually pursuing different things than are couples who meet two years after college when both are working in responsible and roughly equal jobs. Older couples' dreams are different from those of people who settled on each other while still children. What they hope for from one another is different, hence the function of the relationship is different.

One couple grew up in a small agricultural community in the Southwest, met each other before either had entered high school, and were steady dating partners within a few months. The young woman was from the wrong side of the tracks, from a combative family, and lacked most social skills. She was, however, very beautiful. The young man was an athlete, had parents active in community politics, but was very lonely for contact beyond the superficial level. They parented and taught each other through adolescence, over the objections of both sets of parents, and built themselves into each other's psyches as models of goodness and benevolence. Twenty years later when each stopped needing parenting, their relationship fell apart, but their intertwinedness made it almost impossible for them to conceive of life without each other, creating a stalemate that could last thirty more years.

Another couple met on the West Coast when he was in his late thirties and she in her middle twenties, he finishing a graduate degree and she in a vocational training program. Their identities were fully formed, but both needed someone to accept their somewhat unconfident sexual expressions, and each wanted to raise a family. She had no particular wish to parent him, but prized his established ability to earn a living and know the world; he wanted children to parent and sought a functional relationship with someone who could help that happen. Psychologically speaking, these people are fairly independent, far more able to envision life without each other. But they are no more likely to end in divorce, and much less likely to severely damage each other as they struggle for individual comfort and freedom.

For the counselor, a crucial piece of data about any couple is the point each had achieved in his or her own development when the other became a major emotional presence. For many couples, and this is especially true of those in trouble, a marriage is contracted to enable a given spurt of emotional growth, but not to carry people on a continuing pilgrimage. Hence many couples will appear to function at an emotional age a year or two beyond the point at which they finished courting and settled on marriage.

## Our Families Influence What We Want

We come to marriage from families, and those families have greatly affected what we want from a prospective spouse and what we have to offer one, in terms both of technical abilities and personality structures.

People who are good at reading maps do well to marry people who are good at doing business with motel desk clerks, and folks who love to make music are typically happiest with others who like listening to it. Drivers and navigators do well together, as do people whose families taught them to know the ins and outs of retail business, when coupled with partners who learned from their families how to cope with government bureaucracies or university regulations.

The line between technical skill and personality structure is a blurry one. We learn from our families to function adeptly (a technical skill) in a particular role in conversation or relationship, to be those who start the conversations or initiate the relational moves. But when people learn such behaviors fully, as part of fulfilling their family function, the behaviors become part of their habitual way of being—that is, part of their personalities. By the same principle, those who have become very good at listening to others (family members) talk in circles and figuring out what they really mean, will typically have developed a body of expertise and a personality style that favors waiting for the other to initiate, while reserving to themselves the ultimate decision about how the other's beginnings really should be understood.

So we bring from our families a complex repertoire of personal preferences, personality structures, and specific practical skills. Among the most important of those elements are our families' preferred emotions and our responses to them. Some families operate in a very narrow emotional range, and any member expressing strong emotion is either ignored or punished. Children growing up in such families usually decide to act in the only way that lets them remain members in good standing, which is to express emotion only in mild and reasoned ways. Others allow very strong emotions in some registers—for instance, anger—but are very intolerant of strong expressions of tenderness or sadness. Most children growing up in such families will show a lot of anger, but you will never know they are sad. A small percentage of children in either kind of family will, of course, react to the parents' expressed preference by rebelliously refusing to conform, remaining angry in defiance of the parents' inability to tolerate anger or calm in face of the familial expectation that everybody in their family is passionate and loud. That kind of independence is expensive, the children often being defined as not quite in the family; so it usually gives way after a few years, with whatever rebellion remains coming out in other ways.

We also bring to courtship our family's fund of information about the world. Some children move into adulthood well acquainted with public libraries and what's in them, others with a map of their city's bus routes in their heads, others with most of the major Western composers neatly arranged by centuries, others with a detailed knowledge of where to buy parts for cars, plumbing projects, and refrigerators. Each of these pools of information makes us more useful to some prospective partners, and each of the gaps in our information makes a particular possible partner more important for us. If I don't know anything about filing an income tax return, and I find out that someone I am dating has been doing it for years, my interest is likely to increase by a fraction. The combination of thousands of such fractions determines our marital choices.

We bring with us a further vital factor: a direction of yearning, usually to either duplicate our families of origin as completely as possible or to move away from them in a particular way. You often hear of people marrying to get away from home; usually those people want to leave in a particular direction, emotionally speaking. They want less conflict or more warmth or a different kind of expression. But even those of us who felt no urgency about leaving the nest often have in mind some ways we'd like our lives to be different from our parents'. Though those shifts usually are not so dramatic, they often involve a preference for 10 percent more, or less, emotional intensity—for a little greater closeness or a trifle more respect for boundaries; and when we find someone whose own yearning, whose own dream seems to fit with ours, that person's stock goes up a bit.

Though in courtship we are often looking for someone who differs from us in complementary ways, there is a way in which folks who ultimately marry are very similar. Most people choose a partner very close to their own level of psychological maturity, a person whose major limitations come from about the same point in childhood.

Murray Bowen has described this in terms of a scale of differentiation: Persons who are more mature are more completely differentiated from their family of origin—that is, more able to function fully throughout their range of relationships, whether they are in immediate contact with their parents and siblings or not. The more differentiated we are, the more similar our level of maturity, whether our parents are nearby or distant. The less differentiated, the more it will be necessary for our parents to be close at hand in order for us to function competently; or conversely, the more necessary it will be for them to be far away in order for us to appear to be adults. Bowen posits a scale of differentiation ranging from 1 to 100, and states that persons almost always marry someone within 5 to 10 points of the same level on the scale. Further, he says that families move only a few points from generation to generation, so that one of the most persistent family characteristics is the extent to which children are able to function independently of their parents (*Family Therapy in Clinical Practice*, Aronson, 1978).

No one has fully tested Bowen's hypothesis, but whether it proves to be statistically accurate or not, it almost certainly comes close to a major truth. It may turn out that differentiation is not the best measure of maturity, but it is unlikely that the basic contention will be proven wrong: that people find most interesting others who are at about their own level of maturity. If Bowen is right, we just don't click with people who are greatly more or less mature than we are. Their preferred pleasures are a little different, and things we like either bore or offend them.

Another way of expressing all the complementarities and similarities I've just been describing is an old aphorism from an anonymous source: "The rocks in his head fit the holes in hers." Most often, one spouse is just about as healthy or as skewed as the other, with the directions of the skewedness balancing just enough to help each function better as an individual.

### The Counselor Must Learn the History

Once the counselor has a clear idea about what's wrong, how long it's been wrong, and how the couple knew it was wrong—usually around the end of the first half hour in the first session—it is time to begin placing the present pain in the context of the development and concretizing of the original dream. Once the dream and what it meant to the dreamers is known, it is often a simple matter to understand how it began to unravel.

In order to do that, I take a moderately detailed history, spending perhaps ten to thirty minutes on each person, so I can mentally trace the paths they followed as they approached each other. Since the counselor can often learn as much by their selection of what to tell as by the information itself, it's useful to give them plenty of freedom in the structuring of their stories.

So I say, "Now I want you to tell me how you learned how to be who you are. Most people can do that best by talking about the family they grew up in, who was there, what those people were like as individuals, how they related to one another, how you fit into all that, and how it changed over time. Start where it feels right to start, and if you leave out things I want to know, I'll interrupt you with questions." I also let them choose whether to do this alone or together, and who goes first. If there is a reason not to leave that decision to them—for instance, when I suspect there is information I won't get with both in the room—I choose, and we do it separately; but most often it works better to do it together, and that's what most couples prefer. I want them to get used to making decisions as part of the counseling process, and there's no point in the counselor using energy to make unnecessary decisions.

Once the couple starts talking, the counselor needs to listen for specific data. I'm listening for certain facts, and if I'm not getting them, I interrupt and question. I want enough information to get a picture of the personality and place in the world of each of their parents. That minimally includes occupation, level of competence, religious involvement, connection with family of origin, what values they seemed to be pursuing, and the quality of their relationship with the client, then and now. I often ask, "How would I pick your dad out of a group of men about the same age and size?" when I want more data about a father's personality. Ultimately, I want to know enough about all the parents to make a tentative psychological diagnosis of each one, and certainly enough to know how it felt to these once-kids to be with them. It is important to notice which parent they start talking about first, which one they say the most about, and which one they don't seem to know very well.

In the process you will also find the extent to which these spouses are interested in their own families and in themselves. Some families discourage curiosity and personal memory, and their children can sometimes say everything they remember about their parents in about three minutes. When you hit that, you know it's going to be difficult to get that person to look very far inside himself (it usually is a him) for data about the trouble in the present marriage. Others would rather talk about the family history than breathe. If I feel the overload that suggests this person feels better remembering than acting, I interrupt and redirect the flow.

Next, the counselor needs a picture of the marriage of each set of parents. You need to have a feel for the level of intimacy and of conflict, and how the child was affected. You need to know how affection was shown, both maritally and to the child, and also how much and how often anger was shown, and in what ways. You need to know if there were separations or threats of separation. I try to keep working with the data about those marriages until I have a sense of what it would have felt like to be a child in those families. Marriages set a mood that becomes part of the atmosphere the children breathe, and as with the physical atmosphere, if too much or too little of some element is present, it has a powerful effect on those inhaling it. Furthermore, those parental marital relationships are the single most important source of the marital dreams your clients brought to their marriage, either because they wanted their marriage to be just like mom and dad's, or because they wanted it to be very different.

The next bit of data you need to listen for in every such assessment is whether or not there were major changes over the course of the parental marriages—the kind brought about by big financial reverses or gains, job changes, people entering or leaving the household, geographical moves, illnesses, births or deaths, and religious conversions or fallings away. A family's experience is often very different after daddy's business goes bankrupt, or grandma comes to stay, or the family moves from the town where both parents grew up and still know everyone. The meaning of people to each other changes in response to those shifts, and the marriage itself comes to play a different role in their lives. Remember, the marriage starts out with a dream uniquely its own, and when the circumstances change, the same dream often won't provide the satisfaction needed to fill the slot marked "marriage."

Finally, the counselor needs to keep registering data about "What kind of child were you?" It's important to form an impression about success in school, friends, hobbies, and development of competence of all sorts. Keep an ear open for landmark years and correlate these with familywide changes. This is doubly critical when the story reaches adolescence, so you'll need a picture of the reaching for added independence which comes with that stage. Dating relationships and conflict with parents come under this rubric, and it's particularly important to get a sense of the strength and flexibility of friendships formed with persons of both sexes. I like to know about serious romantic relationships before the present one, how long they lasted, how sexually involved they were, how they ended, and what the person learned from them. And if the clients left home before they met the person they're at my office with tonight, I want to know how the leaving happened and how the parents responded.

Those last indicators tell you something of the clients' criteria for relationship before they married, and how those were maturing as they approached the present courtship; and how the clients moved away from the important relationships they had with parents and romantic partners earlier in life. This is especially valuable if there is some doubt that the spouses will stay in their marriage, since it lets you know how bad things may have to get before they give up on something and get out.

By the end of this process—usually by the end or even the middle of the second hour together—you'll know enough about the strengths and needs of the persons to sense what kind of partner each was unconsciously seeking, and roughly where they would have been in the competition for what they really wanted. You also will be assessing their readiness to contract for an adult relationship and learning the shape of the dream each was forming of a prospective spouse and an adult marriage. When you're through asking questions and are ready to put all this together in your head, the couple will need some summary statements from you, to let them know how you're seeing things and give them a chance to correct any mistaken impressions. I try, either at this point or after I've gotten the courtship history, to make some comments about where each was in life at the time they met, and what their dreams for the future were.

I might say, "So by that time, you, Sally, were about fed up with weak men who couldn't compete with your father and were hungry to find someone who could be his equal in your eyes and love you like the mature woman you were; and Bill, you had begun to come out of your shyness and uncertainty about risking yourself and were ready to try to land a woman you really admired. Before you met Sally, you didn't have much competition for most of the women you had been seeing."

If the client agrees with what you say, you look like a genius and your credibility is enhanced, which gives you more power to help them. If they don't think it's quite right, you get to show them you can correct a mistake on the basis of new data, that you can cooperate with them. That looks good, too. In the latter case, keep working with them until you can come up with a wording both you and they agree on, so they can see you are serious about seeing them the way they really are, and you can avoid leaving the session with a strong but false impression of them.

# CHAPTER FOUR

# *C*OURTING
# *AND CONTRACTING:*
# *HOW TO UNDERSTAND*
# *AND INTERVENE*

*C*ourtships that lead to gratifying marriages have much in common with a process of negotiation conducted in code. What is at stake is the agreement to marry, which may or may not be in the interest of the parties. Each has something to offer and each has needs, and no one other than those two knows exactly how important their needs are, or the precise appropriateness of any of the things offered to meet them. Hence the early dating process is a time to find out whether this person is offering the things that fit the other's needs, and whether the things the other can offer are important enough to produce the expectation of a happy life for both of them.

As in any negotiation, it is no tragedy if they decide not to conclude an agreement—that's precisely the right outcome if the needs and interests do not fit well enough. The potential tragedy occurs if the fit is not good, but fear or desperation leads them to pretend it is, and they settle on an arrangement that is ultimately unsatisfying, leaving one or both feeling deceived by the original negotiations.

### Courtship—An Unconscious and Vulnerable Negotiation

James Framo has written that "the choice of marital partner is the most decisive one in life" (*Explorations in Marital and Family Therapy,* Springer, 1982). It is the choice that most determines the environment within which subsequent choices will be made. It represents an implicit contract for both individuals to function at a particular level of maturity, hence has implications for how well either member will do in most arenas of life.

It is also a time of heightened vulnerability to individual pathology and social disaster. The entry into courtship is (for those who don't make a serious investment in athletic competition) the first point where youngsters have to measure themselves against their peers in a major attempt to get something they intensely want. It carries with it three possibilities: failure—the complete inability to establish a marital relationship; success at too low a level—the establishment of a relationship that serves the adolescent hunger to be connected better than it serves a lifetime of continuing growth; or a gratifying and stimulating pilgrimage that will undergird and enable maturation for decades. There are profound differences in outcome, and for some the news is genuinely bad.

Though there are many people who remain single by choice, the vast majority of people want to be married. But by middle and late adolescence it is increasingly clear that for some it's unlikely, or if it does happen, it is likely to be difficult and troubled. Those who remain single out of the inability to establish and maintain close relationships remain at the edge of the herd, where they are vulnerable to predators of all kinds (it has been suggested that mental health professionals are chief among these), feel isolated and unhappy, have less ability to transmit the wisdom that is theirs to others (there being few others who are close enough), don't reproduce themselves, and die earlier.

When we enter that part of life where courtship begins, we all want the validation an intimate relationship provides, and for most of us, that wanting is at times intense, even desperate. But we enter it knowing that some people do not achieve a marriage at all and that many achieve one that is less than we would want for ourselves. So the stakes are very high and the time is short—anyone who falls more than three or four years behind their age peers in developing the skills and habits that typically lead toward marriage has a vastly greater likelihood of not marrying at all. Our knowing all this as adolescents increases the sense of pressure and urgency that makes dating a difficult and troubling experience, though also one that can be enjoyed.

### Dating—Mutual Inspections Through a Romantic Haze

There is an inescapable tension throughout the dating years, as adolescents and young adults attempt to balance their needs for individual maturity, for full knowledge of the potential mate, and for an immediate and intense connection, with what it brings in pleasure and self-esteem.

There is a strong pull to connect quickly, typically felt most keenly by those who are most lonely. Since they are usually the ones with the least developed relationship skills, and often the ones who can least tolerate the frustration of aloneness, they are especially vulnerable. Since these youngsters often are tormented by questions of personal acceptability and see their aloneness as confirmation of their doubts, they often move toward a quick connection—if they can achieve it—to satisfy themselves that someone will really accept them. When the attempt to connect prematurely succeeds (and many adolescents are so socially backward that it does not happen), it can lead in at least two directions. For those whose ability to manage conflict is not well developed and whose sense of entitlement in relationships is easily offended, dating partners may come and go in a series of heavily invested, often sexualized relationships, all of brief tenure. On the other hand, those whose dependency needs are stronger are vulnerable to establishing a very tight bonding at an immature level. These persons will establish a relationship to give them the best of what they see life offering them at age fourteen, and it will go on offering them that until age fifty or beyond.

A second complication of the process is the strong temptation to use it primarily to impress potential partners and to be so preoccupied with whether they like us that we never find out whether they are worth liking. This, again, is a greater danger to the more immature adolescent, with the most frightened and socially inept being so delighted that anyone would have them around that they overlook immense obstacles and abuses. These are the people who, years later, will tell their counselors, "He was the first person who ever paid any attention to me," or when asked the most attractive thing about the other person, will say, "She seemed to like me."

Of course, less seriously limited young people also get caught up in the wish to impress the other, and some impressing is necessary. But it needs to take a back seat to the self-discovery—what really excites and gratifies one in a relationship; and the discovery of the other—whether this particular young man or woman seems able and willing to be and/or to provide it.

The purposes of the processes are simultaneously investigation, negotiation, and competition, to establish whether two people have a compatible set of dreams, whether the same outcomes will be gratifying to both, whether he can give what she needs and she has what he wants; and once someone has decided that the answers to those questions are Yes, then it's up to that one to demonstrate that he or she can do it better or more dependably than the other candidates. But the competition is only relevant and helpful after the other functions have been fulfilled.

As if this were not confusion enough, at some point romantic love enters the picture. Its intense overestimation of the other person makes it even more difficult to pay attention to what we are learning about ourselves and the other. Those feelings often provide enough positive intensity to overcome the fears of vulnerability and closeness that are part of the dating experience, and as such they serve a valuable purpose; but they also can confound and mislead—especially the more immature and isolated.

One of the sources of confusion in romantic love is transference, that universal tendency to project onto the other the qualities and feelings that were part of our relationships with our parents. When we see something in the other person that alerts us that the other is like or unlike one of our parents in an important way, it often triggers the belief that the similarity or difference is much more widespread than it actually is. Typically, a small number of characteristics will produce a sense of safety, comfort, or excitement in the presence of this other that parallels the things that were good about the family of origin; or, for some, parallels the things that were absent but deeply longed for. It's like a "connect the dots" puzzle. If you connect eight or ten dots, the pattern may look like a rabbit or a happy family; but in the more detailed hundred-dot version, it may be a very different picture indeed. Transference is like the eight-dot rabbit, which summons up all the feelings and expectations one has for rabbits, but may not turn out to be a rabbit at all.

At times, transference is very valuable. It steers us toward the familiar, what we know how to deal with; and when intense bonds that feel like being in love develop, they can cement people together in very gratifying and strongly committed relationships. But it isn't a very dependable source of data about another, and its dependability becomes poorer as the pluralism and mobility of our society increase.

The relationships in which romantic love and transference play the greatest part are those in which the intense emotional link to the other happens almost instantly at the beginning of the relationship. Love "at first sight" carries this danger, as do the occasions when someone says they will marry, the moment he or she first sees the other.

Internal object theory, as developed by W.R.D. Fairbairn (*Object-Relations Theory of the Personality,* Basic Books, 1954) and D. W. Winnicott (*The Family and Individual Development,* London, Tavistock, 1965), and applied to marriage by Henry V. Dicks ("Object Relations Theory and Marital Studies," *British Journal of Medical Psychology* 36 [1963] ), Framo, and Clifford Sager (*Marriage Contracts and Couple Therapy,* Brunner-Mazel, 1976), has provided a useful tool for understanding marital transference and its connection with romantic love. The theory is that everyone comes out of childhood with a set of models for both a relationship and a loved one. Those models are based on bonds with parents and other nuclear-family figures, as they existed at different points in childhood. The harsher the childhood, the earlier the age at which those models become fixed. The more benign the childhood, the longer the models remain flexible, modifiable by subsequent growth of the child. A corollary is that the healthier the person, the larger the number and the greater the flexibility of possible models of relationship that can be emotionally invested.

So we may visualize the growing adolescent approaching courtship with these internal models tucked away in the unconscious, functioning as the screen through which all relational experience is viewed. As new people enter this individual's life, the unconscious recognizes whether they do or do not fit comfortably with one of the existing models. If one fits, the possibility exists that this new person can help finish or resolve some of the longing or frustration remaining from the relationship with the original transference object. That increases the emotional relevance of the other, makes what happens with the other more important because it is carrying out a double function—completing some aspect of the old relationship, as well as gratifying the current need for a new one. That gives it a stronger emotional charge, makes the individual more likely to feel strongly toward the other, for good and/or ill; and simultaneously inclines the individual to repeat patterns used earlier in the original relationship (the source of the model) with this new other.

The investment in maintaining this relationship will be greater than in one without this overlay of lifelong feelings, and the likelihood of falling in love is much greater because of this transferential plus. The same internal realities increase both the importance and the intensity of the relationship, and the likelihood that it will be played out in the same old way.

### The Next Step in Assessment—The Counselor Understands the Courtship

When the counselor has learned enough about how these two people became the persons they are, it is time to examine the process by which they came together. This tells you how each chose the other to invest with the individual dream, and how the other allowed it. It gives you a picture of that dream as each saw it and tells you how it became important enough for them to invest a lifetime in it. This process of putting together the pieces from the two individual puzzles is especially important in premarital counseling, when a crucial objective is to help people understand and more fully own their choice of each other. But it is also indispensable in most marital counseling, when the structure of the marital merging often reveals the points at which things need to change.

Two interwoven chains of reality are being sought: the historical chain of events that transformed these two strangers into marriage partners, and the emotional meanings of those events. Since sometimes the second will become evident in the telling of the first, but rarely vice versa, I start with the factual history side.

### The Courtship History

A good place to begin is, "How did you meet?" It's important to push for details of that meeting (and of most of the other things you'll ask about), since you often will hear a very partial answer—"in college" or "at a party." It's especially useful to know whether they were introduced and, if so, by whom. That tells you whether they came into each other's life under someone's sponsorship, which reveals something about the ongoing meaning of the relationship. If not introduced, it's good to know who made the first move to say hello, and why it was made. The context is also important, since it lets you know whether it was a fairly easy situation for establishing contact, or one that required a struggle. All of this gives you an idea about who wanted that first contact, and how intensely it was wanted.

Once you get this first mutual awareness clearly in mind, the next step is the chain of events that led to the first date. For some couples, it was immediate; others may have known each other for years in nonromantic contexts before someone advanced the relationship into the dating realm. In the latter situation, it is vital to know what happened between them that led one or the other to send the signal that changed the relationship. I usually ask how it was decided to have the first date, who asked, why the other accepted, and so on. Again, what the counselor is looking for here is a sense of who wanted the relationship, how much it was wanted, and how much encouragement was needed before a move was made.

Then the process leads to what happened on that date. Though it's good to know where they went and how they spent the time, it's even more valuable to get a feeling for what impressed each of them about the other, and what did not. This is a point at which the continuation of the relationship is tenuous—where a false move could kill it or a chance flicker of excitement could strengthen it—and the counselor needs to know what turned it in a positive direction. After that date is recounted, the counselor should follow up with inquiries about the next steps: How was it decided that there would be more contact? Who called? What were the signals that an invitation would be welcome? Was there any doubt?

That line needs to be followed with an attempt to find out when they knew they were serious about each other and how that was acknowledged. This often dovetails neatly with a question about sexual involvement—how it began and how enjoyable it was. Again, you need to know who made the first move, since by now the pattern of leadership in the relationship should be coming clear, and it's important to know if they followed the same form in the rest of life as in the sexual realm.

This is as good a point as any to inquire about the attitudes of the two sets of parents. The parents no doubt had become aware of the relationship at some point, typically before the decision to honor it in any semiofficial way, and their attitude might have made a significant difference. It is important for the counselor to compare that attitude with what would have been expected from the picture of the parents received in the history. If it does not fit, you need to either correct your picture of the parents or get whatever data are necessary to understand the parents' acting differently in this case. This is a useful principle throughout the process: If new data do not fit with something you had previously learned, be sure you have an explanation for the change, or at least make a note to yourself to be less certain of the picture you had previously held and, when convenient, deepen the data until you find out enough to make sense of the discontinuity.

When the counselor has a picture of the parental attitudes, it is important to move into the decision to marry. I want to know how they decided, who proposed (if anyone), under what circumstances and pressures, and the career of the idea after it first came up—that is, was it accepted enthusiastically the first time it was mentioned, or was persuasion required? Was there only one engagement, or was it on again, off again and, if so, at whose initiative? What did it take to break the engagement temporarily, and what was required to reinstate it? Finally, how was the date set, and what factors went into that decision? If one family had a major role in deciding when it was going to be, the counselor needs to know which family. And is it always the same family that receives consideration, or is there an attempt to keep such things even? The same is true for the rest of the wedding plans—you should inquire about place, size of wedding, handling of costs, and so on.

### The Marital Contract (The Structure of the Dream)

The counselor's next task is to develop a picture of the marital contract, the underlying and implicit set of agreements which provide the support and organization for the couple's dream. Sager's work in this area has taught us that marital contracts exist at three levels: (1) the conscious and expressed—what the potential spouses tell each other about their wishes and hopes for the marriage; (2) the conscious and unexpressed—the hidden agendas each spouse brings into the marriage, the things each hopes to give or get without having to make the giving and getting explicit; (3) and the unconscious—those elements of the exchange not known to the one seeking to achieve them, though they may be visible to the spouse and to others. It is crucial for the counselor to form a picture of the contract at all three levels, since these contracts will provide a clear basis for the behavior of the spouses.

There are several questions you should be asking yourself to test your understanding of the contract. You should know what both parties wanted in the marriage, and how it fits with what they said during courtship and with what they are saying now. You should know what gave each spouse the idea that this other person could help get the thing each wanted. Then, and most important, you should have a succinct and explicit understanding of the emotional exchange, which I often describe as the emotional glue in the relationship. In other words, Who is to do what for whom in this relationship? A typical emotional contract would require a husband to provide a sense of safety, dependability, and structure for a wife, and for her to provide, in exchange, a feeling of emotional aliveness and excitement for him. In every case the contract could be described as the trade of an emotional state which one spouse values and has some difficulty achieving alone, for another which the other spouse values and can't easily achieve alone. The conditions sought are typically the same rewards the spouses came out of childhood needing, which they fantasize they can obtain by achieving a relationship like the model they carry in their heads.

Often the counselor will have a full statement of the emotional contract in mind by the time the courtship history has been finished. The combination of the individual histories and the courtship data will have made it obvious. When that happens, the counselor needs only to state the contract as he or she sees it: "So this is a marriage that was based on your ability to help him develop his independence from his family of origin, to stand on his own with your help, in exchange for his ability to help you feel really connected for the first time in your life, connected both to him and to his family." Always check with the couple as to whether your statement sounds right, and if it doesn't, have them edit it for you. You may not agree, and you may keep the other formulation in your head, but it's important that they see you as willing to modify your ideas on the basis of new data they provide.

Most often, though, there will still be some holes in your understanding of the contract when the history-taking is finished. When that is the case, there are several tacks you can take to complete the picture. Ask what attracted them to each other, what they saw in those early contacts that kept them coming back. If they can tell you something beyond the physical, it almost always is an element of the contract. "He seemed to know what he wanted" and "She was more serious than the other girls I'd dated" are typical answers, as are "He didn't seem to be constantly after sex" and "She was someone I could really talk to."

Sometimes people just stare blankly when you ask them that question, and this requires more counselor ingenuity. The most useful alternative I've found is to ask how the spouse is different from other people each had dated, and if that doesn't pay off, find out whether something happened or each noticed something important about the other just before they realized that this relationship was especially important.

Even if it proves impossible to get a statement of the contract at this point, it is useful to start the spouses thinking about the fact that there is a basic exchange at the core of any close human relationship; then their curiosity can begin to work for you outside the sessions. Ultimately, it is important to be able to formulate what the contract was at the beginning of marriage, how it changed as the marriage matured, and the point at which it began to be insufficient or impossible to fulfill. It is only when that contract no longer satisfies that people experience their marriage as troubled and seek the help of a counselor.

## The Dream Fades When the Contract Fails

As long as both members of the couple feel they are getting what they originally bargained for in the marriage, and as long as that continues to be enough to keep them in psychic equilibrium, the inevitable stresses and conflicts in the relationship will be seen as part of the acceptable price for being close to another human being. But if either of those conditions is not met, they will lose confidence in their ability to achieve the dream the marriage was supposed to be. In that situation, people seek help. The final piece of the assessment process is in place when the counselor understands the breakdown of the contract in the context of the marital history.

### When Did the Contract Fail?

For most couples the wedding was followed by a period when things seemed to be going all right. If you ask them—and you should—how the first year of the marriage went, most of the couples we have a chance to help will tell you that the first few months were a lot of fun, that the trouble didn't really begin until some later watershed.

There are exceptions. The marital adjustment period of six to eighteen months is stressful for almost all marriages, but most couples recognize that as an inescapable fact and don't, for more than a few minutes at a time, see any danger in struggles over schedules, family loyalties, getting to know each other at depth, and negotiating the way the household is going to be run. But there are couples who never resolve those questions, and leaving them unanswered is a persisting obstacle to a full union. When the counselor discovers that that has happened, it is important to go back and attempt the work that was left undone at the beginning; and it will be necessary to find out what interfered with accomplishing it then. Occasionally, couples will seek treatment in those first few months when there have been difficulties, and these are fairly manageable if the counselor provides some communication tools. More serious are the situations where these struggles have not been resolved, but have created a breach that persists for fifteen or twenty years, preventing the marriage from ever getting started emotionally.

There are several predictable danger points for any marital contract, and if the couple cannot identify the point at which the dream began to fade, the counselor will do well to explore the typical ones. The first is the honeymoon, with the difficulties almost always involving sex and affection. If one or both partners have major difficulties with closeness, the couple often finds the first few days of marriage terrifying, humiliating, and terribly disappointing. It no longer is possible to ignore the fear of sex. It is not uncommon for counselors to hear that the marriage has been sexually unsatisfying from the very beginning, with embarrassment or the willingness to settle for less than happiness in that sphere accounting for a delay of years before help is sought. Often after such initial disappointment, the marriage is structured in such a way that sex plays a very minor role, being minimized in importance and avoided when possible. This interferes with both partners' emotional comfort and with the intensity of their closeness, making it easier for the couple to choose either parallel lives or other sources of relational and sexual excitement.

If a honeymoon sexual problem has gone untreated for years, the odds are that major psychological problems are present. Most relatively healthy people either will not have this difficulty or will not tolerate it for long without seeking a remedy. The counselor should trace the disappointment of those first days or hours together to the individual histories and the limitations which resulted from them, while attempting to determine whether the spouses have grown enough to be able to remove the obstacles now. If not, it's likely that fairly lengthy work will be involved, probably requiring significant personality change on the part of either or both spouses.

A second point of danger is the first pregnancy or, in a few cases, a long delay before the first pregnancy. In cases of a long delay, couples usually come in while it still continues, with one complaining that the other just won't decide to have children. Usually it's been agreed from the beginning that there would be children, with a general understanding that this would be delayed until some not clearly specified goals are reached—such as career, financial, or matters pertaining to family of origin. Though one or both parties unconsciously seek to keep this issue unclear, it usually boils down to the fact that someone feels unready to be a parent. Such people are often said to be selfish, but the real issue lies elsewhere. They are, more accurately, impoverished—they feel they didn't receive quite enough parenting and the other experiences of early life to have anything to spare for a child. These are often persons who haven't yet settled into a vocation by age thirty and whose spouses complain they can't count on being heard or responded to in their own times of need. These people are still working on some of the life tasks of adolescence (as adolescence in turn reworks the tasks of ages 2 and 3), and will be grudging and unsuccessful parents unless that can be changed. These concerns, too, especially for the spouse who feels most unready, require a major individual personality change before the marital impasse will give way.

Unlike some of the other typical sticking points, this one will not allow itself to be passed up without being resolved. If people have had a child, it is almost always an indication that this issue has been settled. If they remain childless, with at least one spouse being unhappy about that, this kind of struggle may be in their past, with the feelings about it still needing to be settled.

When a pregnancy actually occurs, the dangers change. The challenge now is to a couple's ability to be both spouses and parents at the same time, which requires the ability to manage a three-party relationship, first in fantasy and then in the flesh. Two interlocked problems are typical here, and some couples have both. Some women turn so fully to their mothering tasks, even in the early months of pregnancy, that they seem to have no energy left to be wives. And some men become so jealous of the actual or imagined withdrawal of investment by their wives that they feel quite abandoned and often turn elsewhere for the tenderness and sexual gratification they would prefer to receive at home.

Most of us go into marriage with some wounds that need healing, and we use the positive side of the first months of marriage to get those injuries tended. In the process, many people hit a growth spurt and feel ready to tackle things in their vocational lives and family development that they didn't feel up to before. If a pregnancy intervenes before that process has been finished, it is a bit like being pushed away from the table while there is still meat on your plate and hunger in your belly. Resentment, anger, depression, and betrayal rise up, along with the sense that something that has been promised is being withdrawn. At that point, some men who have been responsible partners turn cruel, sadistic, and indifferent, which often drives a lifelong wedge into a marriage.

The antidote to the combination of abandonment and rage these men feel is the continued close involvement of their wives. Though there is always some inevitable (and desirable) shifting of the mutual focus to the developing child and the discomfort of pregnancy, in still-thriving marriages, wives show an obvious investment in their husbands' sharing this as part of their own intimacy. It is in marriages in which one or both partners can manage only one relationship at a time (the wife with the fetus, the husband with the wife) that the exclusiveness turns destructive.

The typical disruptions here are either a permanent sexual cooling of the marriage, if the wife continues her tight focus on the children, or the beginning of a string of affairs, or both. Often major and mutual distrust develops, infecting areas of the marriage beyond the original site. Recriminations about infidelity or lack of sexual interest can echo years after this crisis appears to pass. This is a struggle that usually can be helped by working with a couple's communication and tracing their marital history, though some individual work may be required to cement the gains. But it can be done within the limitations of a pastor's time and training.

A similar crisis often emerges with the first move away from the hometown. Many partners find and choose each other while still under the shadow of their parents and surrounded by a circle of friends. In those circumstances they naturally pick a spouse who fits into that milieu, whom those people like and who feels comfortable with them, and who meets the needs that are left over when parents and friends stop providing. Such a relationship often does well as long as the geography remains the same and those relationships remain available. The marital choice has been one way to fit in with those prior relationships. But when the couple moves, say, three hundred miles away from parents and friends, the marriage becomes a much larger part of their social world, and the needs of the partners can escalate explosively. The husband is called upon to provide what used to be obtainable from mom, sister, and the sorority; and most often that isn't what he was picked for. He will find that the things which used to please her are now woefully inadequate, and she will suddenly notice that her standards for contentment and sexual responsiveness have risen much higher. This struggle often happens simultaneously with a much heavier investment in work life for one or both, so that a nonworking partner feels doubly isolated and angry. And if the working partner is perceived as responsible for the move, as is usually true, the anger can reach emergency proportions. Affairs, spending sprees, depressions, and less visible but more lasting desperation to get needs met, no matter what, are typical. A counselor can often ease the pain stemming from such a disruption by tracking back to the time it happened, locating what caused it. The roots usually are intelligible, once unearthed.

A doubly dangerous variation of this dreamkiller is the death of a parent or, even worse, a child. In the first instance, there is the loss of familiar supports and regular fixtures of the social life, plus the much more intense grief of death. One spouse, of course, feels much more disabled by the loss than the other, who still has his or her own needs and ongoing life. The partner's pain requires the other spouse to offer comfort over a prolonged period, while not getting much back from the usual source of support.

Bereaved spouses often suffer a kind of disorientation, never before having lived in a world without the mother or father and not being sure they have inside them what they need to take over the leadership of a family. A paralysis often sets in while they search inside themselves for the resources to undergird their continued functioning. In the meantime, their spouses must go on living, often feeling alone, sad over the loss, but differently, since they have been freed from a competitor for the loyalty of the bereaved.

As with a first move, there is a vast shift in the needs the spouse is expected to meet. The bereaved spouse can no longer expect to receive understanding, financial support, or problem-solving assistance from the now dead parent; and that often creates a demand that the other provide those things, for the first time in the marriage. Furthermore, the courtship was conducted when the parent was alive, so those qualities often were not needed from the spouse. If the spouse does not have them, or is reluctant to make them available on demand, the ingredients for a serious marital crisis are present. The year following the death of a parent is a high-risk time for outside involvements for both parties.

The death of a child is almost certainly the highest risk for a marriage. Both partners are stunned and disoriented, but since no two people grieve identically, they go through the stages at different rates and in different ways. Many bereaved parents see their spouses as not caring in the same way, or as much as they do. That's doubly dangerous if one partner has more or less obligatory commitments in the outside world, and the other does not. Those responsibilities will demand some attention, which the other partner often sees as being withdrawn from the more important reality of their grief. And the spouse who is quickly reinvolved in the world often feels abandoned by the one still actively grieving. The spouse who is ready more quickly to resume an active sex and recreational life can feel alone and in need of stimulation that doesn't focus on the intolerable loss. In that situation, each partner feels that the other is inattentive to his or her needs and insensitive to either the horror of the loss or the need to put it behind them and go on with life. Obviously, the risks of pulling apart and feeling wronged are great. The pastor's involvement in this situation is most useful at the early points, in the first few months after the death. If a year or more goes by and each spouse still is grieving very differently, the breach may be unhealable by any intervention.

A final brand of upheaval that can undermine the marital dream is a major financial change—either a devastating setback or an unexpected windfall. The setbacks are easier to understand and more thoroughly unpleasant, though both are dangerous. The dream always contains an economic element, the expectation that life will be lived at a certain level and that the spouse will be instrumental in helping to achieve it. So the bankruptcy of a business or the loss of a job can leave one partner in default on their marital obligations, and the spouse is faced with the demand for a huge change in self-image and future prospects. Moving from great wealth to modest comfort, or from middle-class status to stark poverty, against one's will and without one's active participation, often produces rage, depression, vengefulness, and the sense of a broken contract, which justifies any and all retaliation.

Shifts in the other direction are more welcome but not less dangerous. Because the dream includes a given economic level, moving to a drastically different level is like having a constitutional convention—everything is open to revision. A contract that seems ideal when both partners envision their future as a constant struggle for economic survival may look very different if that struggle is no longer necessary. It may then seem wiser, and more fun, to seek a partner who is not able to make such an important contribution to the income but is better looking, more fun to be with, or less concerned with making every penny count. Money changes the level at which both men and women can compete for partners, and someone who suddenly can compete for classier company is often tempted to do so. Further, one partner often feels differently from the other about the windfall. It induces a new situation in which one may be inclined to identify with the new-found wealth, while the other would prefer to continue pretty much as before, without incorporating the new financial ability into a changed life-style. Again, the possibilities for growing apart will occasionally produce a breach that a pastor will discover beneath a later marital conflict.

As should be obvious by now, an implicit marital contract that works quite well under one set of conditions may not be tenable at all if the conditions change. A marriage exists in a matrix of nutrients and stressors, and the original dream is crafted to take advantage of the resources the couple expects, and to counter the dangers it knows about. When those things change, the balance inevitably alters, and the marriage will survive and thrive only if it develops new resources or new tactics to handle the threat.

### Why Didn't This Couple Adjust?

No marriage stays constant for longer than minutes, but not all marriages reach a crisis point and need counseling. Couples that usually enjoy their marriages are always amending the dream, developing new abilities to support it, warding off new threats to its continuity. It isn't the magnitude of external threat or change that differentiates successful marriages from those that are not, but the quality and range of tools available to a couple for coping with changed circumstances.

One of two conditions marks couples that end up in our offices: false solutions and failed communications. Either of these difficulties can seriously damage couples' chances to make it to the silver wedding anniversary, and weakness at both levels places the odds seriously against them.

When one of these crises begins to develop, and one or both partners feel the hope in the dream fading, there is a group of typical moves partners use to avoid feeling too badly crushed by the disappointment. They are tried unilaterally and, often unconsciously, provide some individual comfort and/or protection at the cost of the health of the marriage. I call these the false solutions.

The first, and probably the most popular, is triangulation: the turning of major energy to a third party becomes necessary to the emotional balance of the marriage. There are many eligible candidates for the third-party role. The classic is the other woman or man, the sexual partner who provides enough satisfaction, excitement, guilt, and fear so that the involved partner feels life is interesting enough to tolerate. With that in hand, this partner won't rock the marital boat and the status quo can be maintained. Of course, such extra relationships have their own power, which often disturbs the waters more than a little, but that usually is not the intent.

Even more frequently, one parent, usually the mother, turns to a child to gain closeness. This carries the added danger of corrupting the child's view of marriage, since the child feels (rightly) that he or she is the one mommy really counts on and learns that marriage is not a setting in which spouses are close to each other. Many families will transmit this solution from generation to generation, as mother, then daughter, then granddaughter, discover that it is easier to obtain closeness from a child than from a husband; and all have the memory of having witnessed it with their mothers. This prevents marriage from achieving its potential importance and power.

The other classic third party is someone's job—usually the husband's. Since many vocations carry an ideological or financial claim to greater importance than all else in life, it is no mystery that they become as much competition for a marriage as the appealing "other woman." Ministry, medicine, entrepreneurship, and corporate management, especially, tempt their practitioners to believe that nothing is more sacred than the job. That lure is doubly hard to resist if the marriage has stopped pleasing, leaving the approval and success of vocational accomplishment as very tempting.

A final and widely used third party is a parent. These cases are a little different, in that this usually is a problem from the first, if at all, and doesn't wait until dissatisfaction paves the way. But often a couple will seem en route to breaking free into adulthood until some pivotal event, often the birth of a child, reenergizes the ties with the previous generation. Instead of becoming triangles, these are more often rectangles. Young adults who call home every day usually choose partners so involved with their own parents that they don't regard this continual communication as unusual or unpleasant.

A second type of false solution, though it may be considered a special case of triangulation, is physical or psychological disease. Of course, everybody gets sick from time to time, and some people develop severe and chronic conditions completely unrelated to their marriages. But if an illness or series of illnesses begins to be the thing a couple talks most about, or the thing that commands the most interest and energy, it is often being used as a solution to a marital void.

Psychological syndromes are especially useful as counterfeit solutions. Depression, phobic conditions, and hypochondria demand the sort of energy that can keep a marriage under control for a person who feels unable to manage it otherwise. Substance abuse is especially powerful as an equalizer in marriage, since it demands attention on the abuser's terms. Who can ignore someone who passes out at your child's first birthday party or throws up all over the new couch? But physical illnesses can function in the same way, producing a change in contract so that the marriage becomes a relationship for managing the disease, rather than focusing on the overall health and happiness of both partners.

A third kind of counterfeit solution is the decision to settle for half a loaf. People go into marriage with a dream which holds a certain level of happiness to be achievable and requires the efforts of both partners to achieve it. Sometimes, when the efforts of a year or a decade have not achieved it, a partner will give up and decide that what was once thought possible to achieve is now impossible. This partner will stop trying to change things and quietly grieve the dream. This often leads to smoldering resentment or hidden depression and makes it much easier to fall into other false solutions in the years ahead. The alternative is the development of new skills for seeking the original ends, which is a goal and consequence of marriage counseling.

Some tempering of the romantic elation of late courtship is natural and healthy. But this false solution gives up the realistic objectives which the partners set for themselves in the beginning. That kind of goal can't be given up without damage, and in a working marriage, it will be given up only as part of a negotiated compromise which seeks to balance the goods received on both sides of the relationship.

As the counselor hears the history of a marriage, it will often be obvious when and why a false solution was chosen. Equally clear will be the failure of the solution and the process by which one or the other began to realize that such solutions always fail and always cost too much. The task then is to take the spouses back to the point where they chose badly and explore the other choices that were available then and/or might be available now.

The second barrier to keeping the dream current and operating is failure to develop the necessary patterns of talking to each other. People whose marriages remain enjoyable regularly hold conversations in which dissatisfactions are discussed and ways are found to remedy them. Thorough, open communication is indispensable to keeping the contract updated, because the conditions within which it functions are continually changing. With every change an adjustment is necessary if the relationship is to keep meeting needs at the previous level. These adjustments do not happen automatically, and if they are done arbitrarily by one person, without discussion, there is no guarantee that the other person will get what is wanted and needed. If not, the first partner probably will not, either, in the long run, and the solution will fail. Only in a constant sharing of information about how the relationship is working, considering different ways things could be done and sharing assessment of the results of the changes, is there a strong probability that the relationship will continue to be enjoyable over a lifetime.

Most couples that come into our offices have major problems with communication, though that is by no means the only thing that can go wrong with a marriage. A significant percentage of troubled couples will improve as much as they want to, if you help them acquire communication skills they previously lacked, though a remainder do have deeper and more obstinate difficulties. The next chapter will focus on ways to keep the communication network responsive to changes in the environment beyond the marriage, as well as sensitive to the life-cycle changes within it. If you master those skills, you will help the majority of people who come to you.

# CHAPTER FIVE

# *C*OMMUNICATION: DISRUPTING THE DESTRUCTIVE

*I*t doesn't take an act of Congress to disrupt a once workable dream. As we have seen, many processes, both natural and manufactured, can upset the balance of a happy marriage. A change in life-stage, an economic shift, the removal or addition of a key figure in the extended families, an improvement or decline in health, or a change in the hour the children go to school can force a marriage to alter the way it does business.

Since some of these shifts are subtle enough to escape detection, and some are so monumental they can't be digested all at once, there is no guarantee that spouses will immediately realize something has to change. More often they will go on doing things about the way they did before, making only minimal shifts that are physically impossible to avoid. But a few days or weeks, or sometimes years later, it will dawn on one or the other that things aren't working as well as they once did. Usually a mildly unpleasant feeling will provide the first clue. Someone will become moderately depressed or a bit more irritable or anxious than usual. At first the spouses may not link this to the change, but if they sit with it a while, it often dawns on them that the feeling started shortly after the office moved, or Susie's grandmother died, or the youngest daughter started middle school. The longer it takes to identify that feeling and its source, the greater the potential for trouble. Often another shift and another set of unpleasant feelings will pyramid upon the first, before the first has been deciphered. If this continues for many layers, a marital problem that threatens the possibility of the dream itself is in the making. The contract isn't working, and there is danger that one of the false solutions will be tried.

## Straight Talk:
## The Antidote for Faltering Dreams

Only prompt, clear, focused communication can prevent such a change in circumstances from weakening the dream a couple shares, or enable a needed shift from a no-longer-appropriate dream to a new one without major pain or danger.

There are five distinct operations which the couple's communications skills must manage if the spouses are to move through the changes of life without losing hope in their shared vision. *First*, they must be able to utilize feelings as data and achieve mutual respect and recognition for them. This requires a mind-set that regards a change in feeling as important information. People go through their own individual emotional cycles. They move from excited happiness, through calm contentment, toward a modest sadness or even a mild depression, then solve a minor problem and go back to happy, and so on. Each of us has a characteristic pattern. The negative end of our pendulum swings alert us that some characteristic irritation or dissatisfaction has arisen again, so we can institute our typical corrective measures and get things back in order.

But in situations that have the potential to become major marital problems, those measures do not work. The pendulum swings farther in the negative direction than we are accustomed to, or the pattern itself changes, and we get a different unhappy feeling from the one we are prepared for. Those are the points at which a husband or wife can say, "Gee, you've been grumpy lately" or "I just haven't been feeling like myself this week." The couple that uses this transaction profitably will avoid the temptation to hear the comment as criticism or irrelevancy, but instead will routinely take such data as the beginning step in identifying a problem, however minor, that needs to be solved. Once that feeling has been focused, described, and recognized as an indication that something somewhere needs changing, the couple is well on the way to a creative response.

The *second* required skill is that of identifying the precise dissatisfaction that one or the other is feeling. The external change itself doesn't typically cause the distress, but instead calls forth a subtle adjustment, sometimes so automatic it is not noticed, and that adjustment shifts the pattern of gratifications and frustrations ever so slightly. As an example, in one marriage, the children's school schedule changed. Instead of an 8:45 departure time, the youngest child now must be on the bus at 7:00 A.M. The wife, after her 6:00 to 6:30 exercise stint, would like to talk to the daughter. She would also like to be in bed. The daughter comes in, the conversation awakens the husband, who would prefer to sleep. It is not the change in the daughter's schedule that directly causes the husband's dissatisfaction, but the adjustment that was instituted to cope with it.

The skills required here are those of locating the area of the husband's emotional life that had been satisfied before but is not being satisfied by the new arrangement, and of doing it in a way that does not arouse defensiveness or impute blame. In all such cases, someone has noticed an external change impinging on the family and tried to counterchange to restore the fit between the family and the world. It is only when one partner's feelings slip toward the negative that either can know the solution is not a perfect one.

In the situation just described, the link between the change in feelings and the situation that produced it is clear. But that isn't always the case, so a *third* skill is necessary: that of linking a specified change in feelings with a particular change in the couple's way of doing things.

When this skill is in good working order, a couple can go through a process like this: One partner notices he or she is not feeling as happy as before, and identifies a new, atypical feeling. This partner might say, "I notice that I've been sad a lot in the past few days." Then, either together or separately, the spouses will try to understand the sadness, until someone arrives at the awareness that "It's the same kind of sadness I usually feel when I'm going without things I really need"—that is, the feeling is linked with a specific condition of disequilibrium, and with the kind of situation that usually causes it. It is at this point that the third skill comes into play, as the couple scans the recent history for situations of the sort that produce that feeling. They search the events of the recent past until they identify the change that produced the sadness.

This decisive shift must be identified in a way that mobilizes both parties' energy to rectify the situation. If it is labeled so as to make it somebody's fault or to suggest that it was intended to cause pain, then it will be hard to get the other spouse's cooperation in seeking another option. To try to set it straight would be like admitting the accusation. The identification must happen in a way which recognizes that the person introduced the change in an attempt to make things easier or better.

Once that is done, the *fourth* skill is brought to bear: the ability to visualize several different ways to solve the problem (adjusting to the external change), identify the ones that will be tried, plan the process that would be involved in each, conduct the experiment, and evaluate the results. The people with the changed school schedule still need to get the child to school, and the husband's grumpy complaint about being awakened should not end the discussion; it merely identifies the cost of one possible solution.

There needs to be a conversation: "How can we help our daughter feel connected in the morning, without leaving one of us more exhausted than we want to be?" Then some brainstorming needs to happen: We might go to bed earlier; we might decide to drive her to school and sleep those extra minutes; we might look at the scheduling of her time during the wife's exercise, to see whether the great majority of useful contact could take place then; and other possible solutions.

At some point in such a session, the couple needs to settle on one option, and then try it. But they need to avoid committing themselves to this option as *the* solution until they see how it works and have a chance to talk together about whether his needs and her needs and the daughter's needs have all been met by the change. If they have found a solution that meets all those criteria, then the original grumpy exchange will have borne fruit, and things will be better for everybody than before.

The *fifth* step is the adoption of the new solution with such regularity that it becomes a habit. There is a tendency to forget solutions, even good ones, to problems that do not occur often. The next time the situation presents itself, someone may need to say, "Didn't we solve this last week?" in a way that helps the hearer want to remember. A few repetitions of the solution, going through the process in a way that produces happier feelings for everybody, will usually engrave it on the family's consciousness. But the first few applications often need to be monitored by one or both partners. If the solution seems to be forgotten again and again, it may not have been such a good solution after all, and the forgetting may be a way of resisting something that didn't quite work, though those who forget didn't know how to say so. When that happens, it's back to step four to work out a better option.

Most couples willing and able to carry out these steps can handle most changes in their lives successfully and rarely consult us for serious counseling. Though it is possible to communicate well and still have major marital problems, the presence of such problems usually interferes with previously well-developed communication patterns, making it difficult for the counselor to find out what is actually going on until communications have been cleaned up. But straight talk will prevent day-to-day pain from building up into monumental obstacles. If a marriage is severely dysfunctional in spite of good communication, it is almost certain that you are dealing either with individuals who themselves have severe pathology, or with a couple that has gone through a massive

environmental trauma which has triggered powerful responses in one spouse (or in both) that are essentially out of
reach of the other.

## Destructive and Deceptive Talk: The Client's Stock in Trade

When the stakes are high, the people who come to us
usually do not talk to each other in a way that works. Either
they haven't developed such skills at all, or they do have those
abilities but for some reason do not use them in their
marriages. The latter is almost always the case for people who
are fairly accomplished vocationally or have made major
contributions to church and community, since it's almost
impossible to do those things without being able to have solid
and productive conversations with other people. But it is not
uncommon for people who communicate well in business to
regress to less successful levels in their homes.

There is a combination of cultural attitude and marital
contract which interferes with many people's use of
externally developed communications skills for the benefit of
their intimate relationships, especially if the marital contract
itself is largely transferential—that is, if it is based on
expectations that the partner will be very much like (or
different from) a particular parent. Contracts between such
people often contain more or less explicit prohibitions
against clear and intelligible communication. It is common
for a counselor to hear one partner protest that it isn't
romantic to have to ask the other for what he or she wants.
Some people believe that the good deed or the boon received
counts more if they don't ask for it, or if they never need to
make clear what deed would strike them as good.

In other families, though there may be no conscious
commitment to not spoil the romance with clarity, there is a
more quietly habitual routine of handling communication
pretty much the way it was handled in the parental homes. It
typically has not occurred to these spouses that there is any way
to handle things other than the way their parents did. That's a

pretty effective way of dealing with the world, as long as the world doesn't change much between generations. When it does, the repertoire of skills often does not keep up with the demand.

Then there are couples that simply are not used to talking about such things and that are committed to *staying* unused to such conversations. A highly successful forty-five-year-old man highlighted this phenomenon for me recently. We'd been working together for over a year, struggling with the difficulties in his marriage, dealing with his wife's sexual disinterest and his struggle to reawaken it. Finally he came in by himself one night. He said, "I think I've finally figured out what you've been trying to tell me all these months."

"And what is that?" I asked, trying to appear somewhat less eager for the answer than I was.

"That I should work as hard at home, talking to my wife, as I do at the office, talking to my clients."

"That's right," I said.

"I'm not sure I want to do that," he said.

Were it not for confidentiality, I would give that man credit for a great truth, because he said it well. For those of us to whom clear, direct, precise communication does not come automatically, the only way to keep our intimate relationships pleasant and productive is to work at the way we talk in them, just as we do in situations where we're paid to be competent. Without the results this produces, we will not have the ability to adjust the dream when our circumstances change. Somebody's expectations won't be met, and we will have trouble we do not want.

Many people habitually talk in ways that do not have the sharing of information as their primary objective. They are trying to accomplish something by way of protection, intimidation, confusion, or distraction of the other. Many of those methods were learned in childhood, as part of the dominant pattern of speech in a family, and are the methods that come most naturally to the people who use them. But it is all but impossible to use those ways of speaking to regulate a relationship and keep it mutually satisfying over a long period of time.

Virginia Satir, who has had huge influence as a teacher of communications, has isolated four ways many of us speak when we're not talking straight. In *Peoplemaking* (Science & Behavior Books, 1972), one of the classics of relationship literature, she describes them in detail; and in concert with her sometimes colleagues, Richard Bandler and John Grinder, she elaborates them further in their joint work, *Changing with Families* (Science & Behavior Books, 1976). Bandler and Grinder have spelled them out more technically and completely in *The Structure of Magic* (Science & Behavior Books, 1976), one of the seminal works of neuro-linguistic programming. If we are to understand how people fail at communicating, we need to understand these modes.

### Computing

This is probably the most common male method of avoiding straight talk. In computing, the speaker excludes emotion as much as possible from his communication, stating only what he understands as the objective facts. In doing so he eliminates the fact of the emotions he is feeling, or at least attempts to do so. Typically, the chronic computer does not recognize much of his own emotion, does not consider it relevant, placing a higher value on predictability and logic. It's hard to know what is important to these people, and it's hard for them to know what is important to someone else. They eliminate many of the variables that make people unique, hence they often assume everyone values the same things, which, conveniently, will be the things they value— and which they defend as the only possible things that could be valued, since they believe they are being logical in their choice of values.

Computers are monotonous in their vocal tone, lack variety in inflection and phrasing, fail to make much eye contact, and generally sound as though they are reading poorly from an invisible script. They use big words and long sentences, rely heavily on the literal meanings of words, and act as if they do not recognize metaphor and symbol.

Their body style is also distinctive. There is an attempt to separate physical movements and gestures from their speech, so the words sometimes sound as though they are coming out of a statue. They tend to be physically stiff, as if they were restraining themselves from some unwanted movement. They have been trained to favor thinking over acting, and they attempt to make thinking machines of themselves. Hence they rely heavily on data that come in through their ears, in very precise and definable ways—what the more recent writings of Bandler and Grinder call the digital mode.

People who live with computers often complain about the difficulty of knowing how to please them, or the certainty that it won't be possible. Such partners often feel uncared about, disconnected, judged, depressed, and distanced; the computers rarely realize this and, much less often, understand it. You will hear the partners complain that they never know how the mates feel about things, that "He never talks to me," which usually means that he talks only with his head and rarely with his heart. People often complain of not really knowing the computer.

Computers themselves usually complain that their partners do not make sense, that they want unreasonable things which this person does not know how to produce or become. They explain they have said all the things their mates complain of not hearing, and they feel unfairly judged, since they have almost always tried to do the right thing. They see themselves as unselfish and committed, sacrificing their own ends for the things that must be done. People around them become angry at their unresponsiveness, since the computer is so focused on the "objective" data that he misses the other's distress signals at levels obvious to other types.

### Blaming

The second Satir type is the blamer, often aggressively finding fault with those around him or her. These are the persons of either gender who keep their neighbors off balance by attacking their performance or person. They are usually on the offensive, don't listen well or often, and move at a pace calibrated to be slightly faster than that of people around them. So those people feel rushed and bullied, since blamers are often beginning the next accusation before others have a chance to refute the last one. Blamers have a characteristic language style: They are big on absolute statements. You hear a lot of *always, never, worst, dumbest, slowest,* and *laziest* from blamers. They favor the superlative degree and see the world in relatively simple categories. If they like you, you're the best; but they're more likely not to, and then they aren't likely to see any good in you at all.

Blamers typically move their bodies forward and upward, seeking either to get into the space of, or above the other. They often extend fingers, arms, and heads across the other's boundaries, so someone with a blamer often feels pursued and punctured. They tend to speak louder and faster than other people, using a staccato rush of short and simple sentences, often either questions or demands. They don't explain much or see much point in complexity, so they don't sit still for long conversations. In fact, they typically don't sit still in conversations at all, bobbing and weaving in the manner of a prizefighter looking for an opening.

Their relational strategy is to knock the other off their territory, to become king of the mountain. Their language is structured to produce either guilt or fear, and they are most relieved when the other concedes the field. Blamers will resist attempts to get them to produce the rationale for their demands or the authority by which they make them, since they don't expect to hold their own if the other gets the case examined on its merits.

In terms of representational modes, blamers are highly visual. Their language is dotted with visual terms: "Look what you did," "I saw that." They rely on data taken in and represented visually; they value things that can be seen. Hence they make quick decisions on the basis of the first flash of data and often do not look very deeply or notice data that come in through words or feelings.

People in relationship with a blamer will complain that the blamer is angry all the time, that he or she makes them feel uncared about, that they never get a word in edgewise, that the blamer always has to be either right or in charge, and that the blamer devastates the self-esteem of others, especially children.

The relationship between blamer and mate is often hot-blooded, with repeating cycles of accusation, denial, and counter-accusation, or cringing, frightened acquiescence. It has a quality of restlessness, with a pursuer and a pursued, since blamers need to remind themselves of their superiority and safety by assaulting the self-esteem of those around them. Hence the people who stay with a blamer for years tend to feel beaten down and defeated (if they are placaters) or outraged and justified (if they also are blamers). Many blamer relationships do not last long, since this is a style many people try to get away from quickly.

## Placating

The third type is the placater, whose life is structured around preventing the anger of others. Placaters have keenly developed antennae for situations that might upset someone and are constantly reshaping themselves to avoid causing offense. Their communications are full of qualifiers, soft statements that can be taken back quickly or altered just a bit if someone disagrees. It is difficult to trap a placater into a firm and unequivocal stance. Placaters typically bond with persons who don't like to be challenged, hence they often marry a computer or a blamer, whose opinions quickly become the couple's public position. The placating partner is adept at quickly changing his or her stated position, avoiding the appearance of direct conflict with the spouse, yet preserving a kernel of conviction that lies hidden within the broader statements. Placaters are good at conceding an inch at a time, while appearing to always agree with the other.

In Gestalt terms, they are expert at retroflection, doing something to themselves that they would rather be doing to someone else. They reach inside their minds and bodies, rapidly and almost imperceptibly removing obstacles to the views of the blaming or computing partners, keeping whatever anger that self-manipulation causes out of sight, and usually out of their own awareness. So the partnerships are often composed of an apparently leading member, a blamer or computer, who appears either angry or extremely tense; and the placater, who outwardly appears a little subdued or depressed, but inwardly builds a gradually increasing ball of smoldering resentment which often comes out in physical symptoms, depressions, and passive-aggressive behavior.

The physical appearance of placaters often reveals enough to make the assessment simple. Like computers, placaters often appear to be compressed into a smaller chunk of life space than they ought to fit into. But unlike computers, they do not appear immobile and mechanical, moving in response to internal springs or levers; there is more of a writhing, constantly shifting quality about the movements of placaters, with the shifts occurring within a very small space. It's as though they were constantly dodging the thrusts of an assailant, while appearing from a distance not to be moving at all—yet sliding an inch this way, six inches that way, so that the full force of the blow never reaches them. Like computers, they keep arms and legs curled up and close to their center, ready to be used for defense; but unlike computers, those limbs don't appear spastic, frozen, or stiff. They are available to nudge the thrust of blamers a little to the right or left, or to get just a bit of leverage to push against and get out of the way.

Placaters are typically kinesthetic persons, who regularly feel in their gut when danger is near and use that internal physical sense as the major data about what is real in the world. They seem to have a detailed inner record of the physical feelings and movements that accompany different levels of safety, and an automatic connection between those complexes and the moves that would free them of responsibility for the other's anger.

"A soft answer turneth away much wrath."

## Distracting

The last of Satir's conversational types is the distractor, who uses all the modes in rapidly alternating fashion. This person simultaneously attracts a great deal of attention and avoids having to be responsible for any position or behavior. The most important thing to distractors is to not be under the control of another. If a pattern of reciprocal behavior appears to be getting established—in which it is expected that one person will do one thing and then the other will do the next thing the pattern calls for—distractors will feel threatened and quickly shift to another mode to get themselves out of that expectation. These people are very uncomfortable in two situations—when somebody else has gotten them to behave dependably; and when nobody is paying any attention to them at all. Safety for them consists of controlling the other's attention, keeping the other looking and listening while preserving the option of shifting their own direction or changing their own minds.

There are some dependable signs that distractors are at work. They are people who invite your attention to the periphery of things, especially to themselves. They often wear flashy accessories—you will find your attention drawn to the rings on their fingers or their jangly earrings (a high percentage of distractors are women)—and they dress in a fashion that invites attention. A tipoff to identifying distractors is that they are offended if someone responds to their sexual provocativeness with compliments or overtures, claiming to be unaware of their own come-hither signals.

Distractors become adept at shifting modes if they feel in danger of being controlled. They can be very powerful blamers if they sense weakness in the other, but will switch quickly to placating if they feel overmatched. They often have good logical skills, so they can compute when necessary, but generally do so only to confound someone who is trying to gain an advantage by computing or blaming. The shift in mode typically comes just before a transaction is about to reach its objective, so their communication has a "now you see it, now you don't" quality.

Distractors often choose partners who are highly predictable and attempt to control by some combination of careful logic and interpersonal pleasantness—that is, computers and/or placaters. Distractors' liveliness has been valued as a source of variety, but it usually loses its charm as it becomes evident that distractors can defeat, outflank, and confound the less flexible spouse again and again. Just when the spouse seems to have a firm contract, distractors can change modes, angrily blame the more docile partner for attempting to control, then as quickly shift to either computing or placating to start a new cycle. They will typically choose the mode they know the spouse least prefers, wheedling until the spouse accepts it for the moment, then change again when it appears close to producing the resolution the spouse seems to want.

The marriages these people create tend to break down at the point where the early struggles appear to be completed and a stable and satisfying equilibrium appears within reach. Distractors often find this constricting and frightening, and counter by losing sexual interest in the partner, deciding that the partner's vision of their life together is inadequate, or by developing a combination of physical ailments and outside relationships which produce chaos, hence safety, for those who fear being regularized.

### Blocking the Pseudo-Communications: The Counselor's Next Task

Once the counselor has figured out what is going on, has taken the history, and the contract is clear, the main body of counseling begins. The counselor ushers in a subtle transition: "Now that we have a picture of what you want to work on and how the problem has developed, where would you like to begin?" And the clients begin to talk.

Usually, they begin to talk badly. That is, they will use one of the modes of miscommunication we've just described. Your job now is to give attention to the content of their message, but most of your focus in the next few hours needs to be directed toward the way they are speaking to each other. Experienced counselors develop an almost automatic alarm system which alerts them when the communication has slipped away from the direct and useful. Your first task, if that happens, is to shape the flow of words so that it actually conveys data. Once the talk has been redeemed from confusion, deception, accusation, and placating, the air is clear for useful conversation.

### All-purpose Interventions in the Flow of Words

There are a number of tactics the counselor can use that have a good chance of bringing the conversation into a more useful range.

The most widely applicable of these is simple feedback: Tell the clients what you see and hear. It is especially useful to point out the results of a given thing they have said or the way they have said it, or to ask them if they can describe those results. Sometimes it's useful to have them describe the way they said the last sentence, or what was noticed in the partner's behavior during and after the sentence. You are trying to focus their attention on the minutia of their conversational patterns, so they will notice the mistakes they've been repeating without noticing.

You might say, "Did you notice the look on her face when you said that?" "How would you describe the way her body changed when you finished talking?" "Did your remark have the effect you intended?"

With most people, it is not useful to describe the pattern in technical categories, but to focus on specific behaviors, tones of voice, inflection patterns, and vocabulary, linking these with the results they produce. Sometimes it will be fruitful to ask a speaker about the purpose of a particular phrase or gesture, to start teaching the idea that every molecule of communication has an effect, hence a conscious or unconscious reason. Though clients will sometimes find it annoying to be asked to focus on the nuts and bolts of talking and listening, if they are relatively sincere in wanting help, they will soon welcome the power it gives them to improve their relationship.

Sometimes a straightforward rational discussion of the way they are talking to each other won't get through their defenses, and you will need to change your style of speaking to be heard. Often it is a matter of being emphatic enough to pull their attention from the stylized fight they are having to let some new information in. There are several things you can do to break up the pattern and get some attention for what you have to say.

A very usable gambit is to vary your way of speaking from theirs in a dramatically obvious way. On some occasions, that might mean shouting loudly. Or if they are talking so loudly you don't think you can outshout them, try whispering, or singing, or writing a message on the blackboard (a very useful accessory in a counselor's office). Varying the rhythm of the overall conversation is helpful: If they talk fast, talk slowly; if they use long sentences, use short ones; if they speak in monotones, exaggerate the variety of your tones; if they gesture wildly, draw their attention with a gesture and then speak without moving. If the conversation isn't producing, anything you can do to change its tempo gives you a better chance of being heard.

Another option is to vary the task. If they are trying to tell you about last night's fight and repeatedly blaming and computing, resisting your best efforts to get them out of that pattern, you can sometimes take the wind out of their sails with a directive: "We don't seem to be able to talk about that right now. Tell me how your bedroom is decorated." With that kind of intervention, you get the point across that they are wasting their time and that your patience is not infinite.

A different maneuver for such situations is one I call fogging. If people are damaging each other by the way they are talking, and I have unsuccessfully gone through my routine repertoire of ways to stop it, I will often start talking loudly and rapidly about almost anything, preferably something completely irrelevant. My intent is to wrest control of the air from them long enough to break the cycle of recriminations and excuses. Once they stop talking and start trying to figure out what I am saying and why I might be saying it, I gradually slow the pace and lower the volume and maybe throw in a line like, "and I'm going to keep talking until I think it's safe to let you two say something again," and then go right on. I try to end the monologue with a question that returns us to the point, but from a slightly different perspective from the previous one.

One of my agency's favorite stories describes a similar move. A colleague of mine was counseling a couples' group, and one particularly stubborn couple was going through an old argument for the fourteenth time. He tried to stop them, and other group members made attempts and were ignored, so he took off one shoe, then the other, both socks, unbuttoned his shirt, removed it, and was working on his undershirt when the wife turned to him and asked, "What the hell are you doing?" That got her attention off the continuing fight and gave him a chance to tell her what she needed to hear.

A final way of getting a message across when straight talk isn't working is the story or parable: "I once knew a couple a little like you," and the storyteller then details a communication pattern identical to the one the couple is using, weaving exaggerated details into the narrative, letting fantasy take over to produce touches to keep the clients more interested than they might be if you just tell them what's going on. I leave it to your imagination to come up with the myriads of other ways you can take the focus off of a repeated and useless interaction.

### Specific Tactics for Specific Modes

Some of the modes call for specific tactics, and all call for special cautions. Each mode is designed to set up a cycle of exchanges that do not lead toward resolution, and it is crucial that the counselor not be gulled into perpetuating such a cycle.

With computing, for instance, it's important not to try outcomputing the computer. When dealing with a highly intellectual and emotionally invisible person, don't get into lengthy intellectual discussions—especially with the spouse sitting across the room seething. Don't try to abort the cycle by asking the computer a question you're sure can't be answered, meaning to stump the person and stop the evasion. Computers will usually come up with an answer, or deal with not having an answer evasively enough that your tactic won't do any good. There is only one exception to that rule—and it is for very special occasions: When you have decided to beat computers at their own game, you can try writhing around in even smaller details to occupy the computer's interest. Occasionally you can make them cry uncle, but more often you will just lose an immense amount of time.

More fruitful with the computer is to press for the feeling, and to observe how difficult it is for it to come to the surface. Computers will especially hide vulnerable feelings such as fear and sadness. They will often seem more human and approachable if you can elicit a specific fear or regret, though often the first thing to surface, if you scrape a computer hard enough, will be anger, which usually gives way to fear or sadness. If you can get through the sometimes intimidating anger to the other feeling, you can often effect a connection for yourself or for the spouse.

Also, it often makes computers approachable to point out their inevitable investment in being right, perhaps even getting them to wax eloquent about the virtues thereof. Then you can ask if being right so often is making them happy, knowing that if it were they almost certainly wouldn't be in your office.

As a further computer-confounder, challenge the criteria the computer is applying and continue to suggest new ones until confusion is so rampant the field begins to clear for whatever else you want to do. Computing depends on an absolute standard of right or wrong, so if you can render any such standard relative or absurd, you have knocked computers off their pedestals and have created, however briefly, a situation in which new learning is possible.

Blaming is also susceptible to specific countermoves. Bandler and Grinder suggest that the counselor "play polarities" with the blamer: If you can blame better than the blamers, the blamers will always shift into their secondary mode of communication, which will usually be preferable to the blaming. So one countermove you can always use with blamers is to be a bigger blamer yourself, using all the tools that make blaming work: make vertical physical moves, move intimidatingly into the blamer's space, use absolute statements—pushing for guilt or any other emotion that would put a drag on the blamer's power. This is a last resort, but it does work and is fun for both the counselor and the other spouse.

When the blamer has started blaming, it is also very useful for counselors to assert their own authority, without blaming, especially if the blaming is directed toward the counselor; this can also be done if it is directed toward the spouse. There are two ways in which the authority can be claimed. The first is by moving directly to stop the offending behavior: "I can't let you carry that on in here, it's too harmful"—this can be escalated in volume and length if necessary. The second way is to use your central role to direct attention not at the content of the blaming, but at the feelings it's coming out of: "You sound that way a lot, especially when you talk to him. Have you wondered why you use that particular tactic?" "I've noticed that when you say that you use about three times as much voice as necessary. Do you know why you're doing that?" That question essentially uses the authority of the counselor to redefine the task, blunt the blaming, and keep the heat on the blamer instead of letting it be shifted to the spouse or the counselor.

As is true with the computer, the blamer usually is hiding feelings. Pushing for the hurt, sadness, or fear that underlies the readily available anger can often change the transaction abruptly: "Someone must have hurt you very badly for you to be so hurtful now." The blaming has to slip only briefly to cease being a flawless cover.

## *DISRUPTING THE DESTRUCTIVE*

Especially at first, it is important to shore up the blamees during such a transaction, so they won't experience the counseling as intolerable. It isn't necessary to agree with them or defend them, but after an attack you can ask them to restate what the blamer has said, think over what they agree with, and decide with you how they are going to respond. As you interpose yourself between the blamer and the sometimes helpless attackee, you change the equilibrium and make it obvious that blaming will not have its usual entertainment value for the other.

Finally, you can challenge blamers' thinking head on and ask them to defend it. Usually the blamees are so angry or injured that they don't think through a blamer's attack, and if you demand that the charges be substantiated, you will often knock blamers out of that stance by forcing them to reflect.

"Induce thinking" is also a good rule with the blamer, especially once the blamer has decided to respect the counselor.

With placaters, the crux of the counselor's response is to identify the fear(s) that keeps the placater from asserting. Usually it will be a fear that stopped being realistic many years ago, since placaters are much harder to destroy now than they would have been at age 3 or 5 or 7. Track that down any time you catch placaters doing their thing.

Sometimes it's important to push the placating to its extreme, because even placaters have a point they won't be pushed beyond. Once you have done that, you can say to them that the dreaded danger isn't so great that it's worth being pushed beyond position X; so let's look at whether it's so great that they would also choose to abandon this earlier position, and this one, and this one. Ultimately, it is necessary to point out the long-range results of placating. They never get what they really want, and they still can't be sure of the other's loyalty or that the other won't hurt them the next time. They never get away from the knife edge.

Another useful intervention with placaters is to remind them how lonely their partners must be, since a partner never gets anything back from a placater other than what the

*9 3*

placater thinks he or she wants. Nothing ever comes back that is uniquely that person's own. Reminding the placater of that fact frequently, plus being visibly available to prevent harm from the partner, will help the communication get more lively.

The secret with the distractors is to catch them in one mode and not let them escape until they bankrupt themselves in it. If it's blaming, keep them in blaming until they have to back down. The other important key with distractors is to watch out for seductions. They will often try to move you from mode to mode, looking for the one in which you will be malleable. It's important to give as little response as possible to distractors, thus maintaining their uncertainty about how you can be conned.

If you can dependably identify and label these crooked modes of communication and stay out of their reciprocal cycles with clients, you can fairly quickly condition clients out of using them as their dominant modes of speech. When that is done, much of the hardest work of counseling has been completed, and you can get on with the more dependably productive hours. It will always be necessary to come back to these tactics, since new stresses will reintroduce old defenses, but once couples have learned to rid themselves of these games, it will be easier with each new recurrence.

# COMMUNICATION: EMBODYING THE BEST

*Y*our most powerful communication-related act is to serve as a model of straightforward communication. No matter how well you teach good talking and listening skills or obstruct unproductive patterns, if your ways of getting ideas across do not provide patterns clients can follow, your impact will be dulled.

Your clients will copy your ways of talking if they find them helpful. This aspect of counseling is an informal conditioning process, in which a set of language patterns that increase a couple's power to get satisfaction out of life is being learned. If clients notice that their spouses respond differently when you talk with them from the way they respond when they do, and they notice how you do it, they are likely to give it a try.

The odds are that if you are kind, clear, and get results, clients will feel better. At first that may seem magical to them, but you can clear up the haze by directing their attention to your method. "Did you notice I asked my question in a slightly different tone of voice from yours?" or "I tried to phrase my feedback in a way that wouldn't encourage a person to become defensive." They will link your way of talking and their way of feeling, and will begin to imitate your patterns of speech.

The great majority of clients will get some benefit simply from the bracing effect of being with someone who talks straight, though a few holdouts will almost glory in the ability to resist being thus affected. More about them later.

## The Counselor's Communicative World

The way the counselor talks and listens creates a world that opens new possibilities for the client. Through your modeling and teaching of a style of conversation different from the one they learned in their homes, you create safety for exploration, experimentation, and self-expression that will become the soil in which their relationship can grow.

In her four modes of communication, Virginia Satir described the styles we have discussed. All fail to provide their users with the best chance to be happy and productive. She also describes a fifth mode, which she terms "talking straight" and recommends as the best way to build one's partner's self-esteem and, ultimately, one's own.

The stance I prescribe for the counselor is an expansion of Satir's "talking straight," typified by the ability to look the client straight in the eye and say exactly what that counselor means; then to watch and listen carefully to be sure it has been heard as intended. The repetition of those acts, over and over, creates a different atmosphere from that in which most clients have regularly lived. They have learned a style of non-straight talking to help them survive in a world very different from that of the counseling; hence entering this world creates a safety which, in turn, calls forth new flexibility.

The first word to describe the counselor's communicative world is *congruent*. You are congruent when the feeling (emotion) you have inside is the same as your conscious idea of that feeling, and the same as the way you look and feel to other people. It suggests an absence of self-deception and other-deception, sameness all the way through, which allows the other to sense what will be safe in your presence.

The word and the emphasis come from the work of Carl Rogers *(Client-Centered Therapy,* Houghton-Mifflin, 1951, and the movement of the same name), which was central to the development of pastoral care and counseling in the 1950s and 1960s. That movement contends that a necessary part of counselors' skill is the knowledge of their own feeling almost all the time and the knowledge of how that feeling developed. The feeling should always be available to the counselors as data about what is going on in the room. It especially means that counselors will not deliberately deceive the client about their feeling, so that the client can gain the experience of working in a feeling context that is increasingly clear and intelligible.

The need for congruence forces one major problem upon counselors in general. Some feelings we may have towards clients will hinder the work or be flatly destructive. If counselors try to hide these feelings, two difficulties are created: it doesn't work; and insofar as it does work, it disrupts a counselor's congruence, which will show up as a distortion in the counseling relationship—a stiffness or distance that interferes with effectiveness. The only remedy is for the counselor to do something to change the feeling. If it is an infrequent emotion which seems to arise from the immediate situation, it requires immediate action to change that situation (such as blocking a behavior that has led repeatedly to the counselor's becoming angry). If it is a feeling that develops often with a variety of clients, it represents something unfinished in a counselor's own maturation and calls for the counselor to take it up in his or her own therapy and/or supervision.

One of the great blessings and great demands of this work is that it confronts us with these weaknesses and gaps in our own personalities and forces us to grow to fill them, if we are to be effective.

A second quality of the counselor's communicative stance is its *attentiveness to the client's self-esteem*. People come to us feeling vulnerable, often feeling that the coming itself is a shame that will be hard to live down. On top of that, the pain in a couple's relationship has raised doubts about the spouses' ability to succeed at their most important human bonding. Often the messages within that relationship have encouraged them to doubt themselves further. Human beings in that situation usually retreat to their oldest, best-established methods of protecting themselves, which are almost always full of obstacles to growth and self-revelation. They will join in the self-exploration required for growth only if they trust that the counseling will not deliberately assault their self-esteem, thereby lowering it further.

When people are low on self-esteem, they are exquisitely sensitive to further dangers to it, so we must become expert at avoiding accidental wounds to the clients, and must purge ourselves of those motives that would inspire deliberate wounds. We must learn to avoid any action that makes clients feel incompetent, so one of our most important assets is the ability to create a situation in which clients know what they must do to succeed, and then maintain that structure systematically, so that when clients do the things that are prescribed, they actually do succeed.

There is a wide range of counselor behaviors that make a difference to the clients' feelings about being in the room. Clients must feel our respect for them, and they must be helped by us to experience their own respect for themselves. All the things that communicate respect in a personal relationship operate here, plus other elements peculiar to the professional nature of the work: tone of voice, choice of words, fitting one's vocabulary to that of the client, handling of interruptions, respect for schedules, seating arrangements, and so on.

The counselor's communication must also be *transparent as to goal.* That is, we must be as clear as possible about what we are driving at, why we want certain information, the point of having this uncomfortable conversation, and so on. This is part of being attentive to the clients' self-esteem. It communicates that the clients are persons who would not be subjected to this discomfort, were it not for some shared purpose. Further, when we give advance notice of where we are taking the conversation, it often stimulates the clients' thinking, so they will get there before we do, saving ourselves and the clients a lot of time and discomfort. It also helps to create a sense of the logical connectedness of events in their marriage. If we start from point A and announce our intent to go to point D by way of B and C, they begin to get the idea that they can predict the consequences of their actions in the relationship.

Another crucial characteristic of the counselor's communication is *persistence*. When you see something that needs to happen in the relationship, don't let go of it. Either get it to happen or make them demonstrate that it won't happen, no matter what you do. Many couples get into worse trouble because the spouses start a conversation that is desperately needed, but are frightened into stopping before it reaches resolution. One function of the counselor is to buffer them against this fear and provide the will to push the conversation through to the achievement of its task. The counselor must not allow vital interests to be overlooked or let mild anxiety abort a process that is going in a productive direction.

This is more than sheer stubbornness, though sometimes that helps. It involves the skill to know when a conversation is necessary, and the ability to identify the barriers that prohibit carrying it to conclusion. Often a couple retreats from a conversation to protect one or the other spouse, when what is needed is a quick discussion of the fear that is tempting them to stop, a reality check as to whether the actual danger approximates the one fantasized, then a prompt return to the subject at hand. The willingness to bring them back to the point again and again is a vital personal qualification for marital counseling.

The counselor needs to be *emotionally intense* enough to counter resistance. Unlike individual therapy, in which almost any emotional assault on the therapist can be sidestepped, there are times in marriage counseling when the counselor must either stop something that has started to happen, or force something to happen that won't happen without the counselor's investment. This often requires that you be as loud as they are, as grim as they are, as immovable as they are. Your way of using yourself in the room must communicate that you are willing to bet yourself, your energy, your reputation with them, even your professional dignity, on the importance of stopping a destructive process or advocating an indispensable one. Obviously judgment is crucial here, and if you are going to lay yourself on the line, you'd better be right most of the time. But being right isn't enough by itself—the marriage counselor must be prepared to be right in a loud voice, or with tears in the eyes, or while standing between a fleeing partner and the door. And clients must trust that you will not stand by and allow them to damage themselves or each other.

You must be *curious*, yet respectful of needed privacy. A crucial belief for a counselor is that any new information about the people you are with is likely to be valuable, so when a question comes to your mind, ask it. It is almost always true that more information is better than less, though it also is true that some information is more important than other. A dependable guideline is that once the story of an event is begun, it is good to carry it through to its finish, unless it is obviously damaging one of the parties. If they try to stop in the middle, and you see no reason for stopping, act interested in how it ends. Usually they will be flattered, and at least they will know you are awake. Furthermore, you are teaching something: that the more the two of them know about each other, and the more you know about them, the more likely you and they are to understand and like one another. Your visible expectation that the development of information is likely to be more pleasant than painful is a powerful teaching tool.

Another facet of the counselor's world of communication is its *playfulness*, its permeability to the unconscious of both clients and counselor. My best work is done at points where it is closest to play. Most couples come to a counselor deadly serious, and part of your function is to restore the ability to play, to play toward a shared objective. The more strictly serious any of us are, the more we are limiting the percentage of available knowledge and energy we can bring to bear on a problem. An ideal paradigm for marriage counseling is a counterpoint between the moments when the wildest fantasies, wishes, and daydreams are fed into the process as data, and the more reflective, pensive times during which the three of you are thinking out loud about the meaning of what has gone before.

A final element of the counselor's world is *attentiveness to contexts*. Each moment in a counseling hour occurs in a multiplicity of surrounding circumstances, a complex matrix of environments; and those contexts determine the meaning of the moment. They are the hermeneutical key to each bit of interaction between husband and wife, or between either spouse and the counselor. To be trustable and therefore effective, you must discern which of the possible contexts is the most meaningful and must communicate that to the clients. When that happens, clients feel that their experience is being taken seriously and that it's safe to reveal and experiment.

The most important context is the ongoing relationship between the husband and wife since you were last together. It is indispensable that counselors develop ways of sensing, in the first few moments of a session, how that intervening time has changed the relationship. A standard flip greeting or a narrowly focused continuation of last session's agenda will flounder, often dangerously, if she has just run over his favorite hunting dog or he has recently been discovered in a passionate embrace with her sister. Similarly, agendas that were appropriate last week may be quite out of place if extended family events have altered the couple's priorities. The death of a parent, a newly discovered plan for a visit from in-laws, or the serious illness of a child or sibling can appropriately produce a change in focus for the counselor. If that is missed, energy will quickly dissipate in the session and the clients will feel that their actual concerns are not being engaged.

Another context to which counselors need to pay close attention is the physical one—the place they are meeting the clients. The rules are different if you are meeting in your office, in your home, in their home, and so forth. Different kinds of offices create different contexts: Privacy is more or less complete, interruptions more or less probable, secretaries more or less discreet. Any different setting indicates slightly different behaviors: You can move more firmly to prohibit interruptions in your office than in your home, and in your home than in theirs; you can offer or get a cup of coffee in your territory, but not in theirs; you can pick your chair and assign theirs at the church or in your house, but you'd better be respectful of the family's preferred seating if you are on their turf.

Geographic contexts are also important, since the meaning of both marriage and seeing a counselor is different from place to place. Marriages typically play slightly different roles in the lives of people in the county-seat town, where I live, from those in the urban center twenty-five miles away, where I practice; and it's a little different there from the major metropolis a few hundred miles away, where I trained. And it would be different still on either coast, or in parts of the South. Each community has its own subculture, often varying significantly only a handful of miles apart, with expectations and standard behaviors differing enough to trip up the counselor who assumes them to be the same. Fitting the context correctly would show up in behaviors such as showing the proper degree of familiarity or distance; knowing how much equality between men and women you can assume; and understanding which events between a husband and wife are typical and which are exceptional.

A couple's theological context is another important concern for the counselor, especially when it comes to language, since members of some faith groups recognize a helper who can be trusted by certain words and phrases and are equally likely to rule out someone who uses language foreign to them. If you have language that's comfortable for you and fits with the people you're seeing, it's valuable to let that show, especially early in the process. It often helps the clients to see you as a person who shares their basic commitments. This is one advantage pastors have over nonclergy counselors—they often know in detail what options will be acceptable to members of their congregations, and which *cannot* be offered or considered without jeopardizing credibility with the client.

Another critical context is that provided by the couple's position in the life cycle. Events have different meanings in the first few weeks of marriage from those they have thirty years later. Priorities change when children are born, when they go to school, when spouses are promoted to responsible positions in their vocations, when children reach adolescence, when aging parents fail, and upon retirement. Most of us can't completely predict the objectives of someone in a quite different stage of life, especially one who is further along the journey than we are. It's important to let clients teach you about their life stage, and to let them know they are teaching you. Assuming that the same things that are important to you are important to them will get you in trouble.

A particularly important piece of this context is the maturing of the communication pattern in a marriage as it ages. With newlyweds or couples in their first few years together, a counselor can often be helpful by translating what one is saying, awkwardly and imperfectly, to the other. Their own communication channels are still flexible and incomplete enough that saying it a different way, for the purpose of clarifying to the husband what the wife is meaning, will be a genuine assist. But the same husband, twenty-five years later, will, in most cases, know better than you what that slight change in inflection at the end of the last sentence meant. They've had decades to practice delivering and receiving subtle messages and can often carry on complex conversations in your presence of which you understand only the surface level. Trying to translate the meaning from one to the other in a mature marriage is risky at best, and often leaves the counselor looking foolish, having inadvertently revealed that he or she doesn't really understand the code. Better to ask and let them tell you.

With regard to contexts of all kinds, the crucial element is that you communicate your awareness that the clients live in a set of circumstances that you know only incompletely. They know that already, and if the counselor claims to know more fully than it is possible to know, the counselor stands to look like a fool. It's crucial that counselors acknowledge to clients that any given act or word the three of them share could possibly have relevance to a huge variety of possible situations outside and inside the room, and that it is largely up to the clients to let the counselor know which context they deem most important. This makes it clear that the counselor respects the clients' sovereignty over their own lives. Failure to do this appears as a challenge to that sovereignty, which inevitably creates anger, distancing, and resistance to the work the couple has come to do.

## The Counselor—Explicit Teacher of New Skills

By establishing such a communicative world, the counselor has been implicitly and indirectly teaching. The learning occurs through the clients' experiencing a different environment, a different context from the one they have been used to, and finding they can safely use different behaviors in that context. It is learning by experimentation. But if you asked clients at what moment they learned how to be more congruent, or attentive to a spouse's self-esteem, they usually couldn't tell you. They have gradually internalized a different way of communicating with other people and, it is to be hoped, introduced it into life with their spouses.

But another major teaching method in marriage counseling is explicit and direct. Some of it proceeds by question, as when you ask clients a question which leads into a subject they usually don't talk about. Some of it proceeds by direction, as when the client tries to change the subject and you bring the conversation back to the subject that needs discussing. And some of it proceeds by direct instruction, as when you point out the lawful connections between "I messages" and feeling responsible for the outcome of a conversation.

This is the aspect of counseling work that moves quickly, not waiting for the counselees to get the idea of a different behavior by copying the counselor. Such teaching builds in specific pieces of knowledge clients know they have, and which they can go back to if they temporarily lose track of the feeling they want or the style of interaction they'd like to create. Though your creation of the communicative world is an intervention, it is a global one. But your more specific interventions, the direct teachings, proddings, questionings, and blockings, are the things that mark your power to have an impact that is more focused, problem-specific, and powerful than mere pastoral presence needs to be.

## The Basic Setting—
### Conjoint Three-Party Interaction

The best counseling structure for maximum marital impact is the conjoint setting, with the counselor and both spouses present, because it recreates the situation in which the spouses must become effective. Ultimately, you know how well or badly you and they are doing in the counseling only by what you see and hear while they are together. Anything one of them might learn in any counseling setting must be tested with the spouse, over whatever objections or resistance that other may have. So it makes sense to begin in that setting and continue in it until something makes you change. Usually you will not change, since those are the therapies that work best and move fastest.

There are several other advantages to the conjoint form. One of the most valuable is that it gives you access to information when you need it and a way to check out that information, verify its accuracy, which you would not have if the spouse were in separate sessions (concurrent counseling). The safeguard exists because neither spouse can say things the other thinks are untrue without the other objecting, so if something is presented as a fact and nobody complains, you can be fairly sure of it. Furthermore, the setting gives you new information. Many times you will be talking with one spouse about the development of an event and reach the point where you need to know a bit of data about what happened next, or why it happened, or how it looked from the other side of the room. If the other spouse is there, you can ask. You have the advantage of being able to construct a version of events from the standpoint of the information available to both, without the lost time and the danger of misunderstanding that can happen when you carry one spouse's version for hours or days before you have a chance to compare it to the other's.

A further important plus for conjoint work is that it provides access to the motivation of both parties. Often a spouse who refuses to talk with you alone will be glad to come in to challenge the partner's expected misconceptions, or to try to get the partner to change. The conjoint hour gives each a chance to speak to the other with someone present to referee, to translate, to enable; and people will very often see an advantage in stating their concerns to a spouse when they do not have any wish to change their own behavior. Of course, for the counseling to succeed, both parties must change; but the process is often far along before both spouses see that.

There are, however, some situations in which concurrent counseling works better. When it's unclear whether both parties are committed to working on the success and maintenance of the marriage, the counselor needs to find out. One spouse often will not be honest about that in the other's presence, especially if there is third-party involvement, or if the partner who does not want the marriage is addicted to being agreeable. In either case, that partner will let you continue to assume you have a shared contract—unless you create a situation in which it is safe for the person to tell you. Once you get that information, you have the problem of how to use it; but that is more manageable than trying to conduct counseling on the false assumption of shared commitment.

You will also need to see partners separately when they behave so destructively together that the counseling does more harm than good. People must experience the counseling as a safe place, especially at first; and if it becomes a place where one spouse hurts the other more than at home, they won't keep coming. So if the spouses are damaging, not just making each other uncomfortable, and it serves no useful purpose (such as generating information you need), and you can't control the level of conflict, it's time to separate them. The level varies from one counselor to another, since all of us differ in our ability to manage and direct our clients' conflicts, but it is crucial not to give them reason to believe they are less safe from each other in your office than at home.

There is another condition under which you would do well to see partners separately: When you suspect there has been an agreement (or demand) not to share certain information with you, or when it seems likely that information from the sessions is being used against a spouse between times. You find out about this from gaps in the conversation, which sometimes will be filled if you say there seems to be something missing: or if you comment that most people wouldn't come for counseling unless something more were wrong; or if you ask what prompted them to define the situation as serious. If none of these suggestions jostles anything loose, tell them you would like to spend one session with each of them alone, or perhaps split a session (half an hour with each), to see if that will help you resolve your confusion about their situation. Then, in the private time, you can say that sometimes this confusion crops up when people have decided to keep part of their lives secret from the counselor. If you have a hunch about what the information is, it can be valuable to say so, while clearly identifying it as a guess, and perhaps even suggesting why they might want to keep it from you, if you think you know. If you get new information, you need to work with the client who shared it about how or whether the other spouse is to know. You can use it in either event, but things generally go better if everybody has the same information.

### *The Objective—Completing the Conversation*

The longest and most productive part of counseling, starting even before the assessment is finished and lasting almost until the end, is a series of conversations between the spouses, with the counselor serving as intermediary. Your function is to help the couple have the conversations that have been needed, but, for whatever reason, have not been happening.

Some of this is done by simply setting the hour and providing the space for husband and wife to be together, with their relationship as the agenda. Once they are together and you have asked them what they would like to work on that day, one of them will usually introduce a topic that needs to be discussed (in a troubled marriage, almost everything needs to be discussed at least once). In the early part of the work, most of your attention will focus on gradually purging the discussion of the games and deceptions discussed in the previous chapter. Eventually these will give way—first, for a few seconds or minutes at a time, and later, for whole sessions at a time—and a real subject will be on the floor, ready to be seriously engaged.

Since all such subjects ultimately lead to the heart of the relationship, all, if pursued, will be valuable. The problem usually is that conversations haven't been pursued far enough at home, so the couple believes that raising serious issues makes people uncomfortable but doesn't help solve anything. So they have quit talking, at least about important things. That is the cycle the counseling must break, so that when they are finished they will know they can have an effective conversation about any subject and that enough will be gained from it to be worth the discomfort it causes.

The cycle is broken by providing them the experience, again and again during sessions, of raising issues and talking them through, so that everybody understands what the problem is, how much it matters, how it came to exist (and in whose interest), what the alternatives are, and which alternatives provide the best balance for mutual advantage. It is even more useful if these discussions can end in clear contracts about how things are going to change, who is going to do what differently, and how they are going to handle it if one of them thinks the other isn't holding up his or her end of the bargain. When a couple can have that kind of conversation about any issue, life will soon be much more enjoyable for both spouses. They are nearing the end of their counseling.

Most conversations that do not reach that end fail because they have not lasted long enough. They have gone off the track somewhere, and instead of retracing their steps and getting back on line, the spouses give up, breaking off the conversation or changing the subject. They don't know what to do next. Their communication skills get them to a point about halfway through a conversation and strand them there, unable to reach the end. In frustration, often blaming each other for their distress, they stop the flow or trivialize the conversation.

The most decisive contribution the counselor can make is to provide new behaviors for moving beyond these impasses. It is crucial to do something to keep the conversation alive and move it through the tension.

One dependable gambit is to ask either partner what he or she is feeling—either about the partner or about the subject they were just discussing. The answer provides new data to which the other can respond. If the person does not respond immediately, you can ask for a response. "Bob, did you know she was feeling that way about this? What does it mean to you that she was?" This move is especially useful if either partner was feeling something strongly, obvious to you, but not said out loud or acknowledged by the partner. You will often find that the other partner expected a completely different emotional state, and that the surprise produces a change in the other's feelings.

Another move that is useful, especially in a conversation that was going well until it stumbled, is to ask them to give each other feedback on the way they were handling themselves before the conversation stalled. "Jane, could you think back about 60 seconds, when Bill said what he did about your son, and tell him how you were responding to the *way* he was saying that?" Obviously, this is most useful when you have noticed something in her behavior that will help the conversation. Once she has spoken, you can ask him about his response to what she says.

If you suspect the reason for the impasse is confusion about what one or the other means, you can push them both to be more specific. One confusion that more detail can resolve is knowledge about the intensity of a feeling. Each needs to become expert at knowing how much something matters to the other. If one is complaining of being "upset" by something the other did or said, get the person to focus on "upset" until it's more identifiably "angry" or "hurt" or "disappointed" or "surprised," and preferably until the other could accurately rate that emotion on an intensity scale. Then people know what they're up against.

A further possibility, if you hit a period when neither will volunteer anything, is to ask one or the other why he or she is not speaking. By doing that you're trying to get information for both yourself and the spouse, to give the spouse a start at providing feedback that will be routinely valuable. A good time to ask this is when the last thing the other said leaves little room for response. If you can get the one who did not respond to say why, you can then ask the other if that was the intended effect. It usually wasn't, at least consciously, and the exchange will help the couple focus on an often repeated transaction that is regularly frustrating. Many couples have recognizable ways of shutting each other off, of saying something that makes it impossible to respond. Often the couple is not conscious of this, and if you can identify these automatic conversation stoppers and help the couple recognize when they are typically used, you can enable the spouses to gain control that may lead to their removing those behaviors from their repertoire.

A completely different maneuver is to share something of your response to the conversation. That can be done in several ways: You can share your feeling, you can lay out a fantasy you are having, you can tell a story. Whichever you do, you will be promoting meta-communication, communication about communication, getting them to look at the way they are talking, rather than at the content of that talk. You might say, "While the two of you were having that conversation, I found myself thinking about two little kids hiding behind great big boulders, throwing raw eggs up over the boulders, each hoping to land one on the other, but never even coming close." It doesn't make too much difference how precise your image is, but it must be interesting. If it attracts their attention, they will correct for whatever error is in it, and you will have lured them into thinking about the style of their interaction.

A final but particularly important tactic is to block their attempts to move away from the impasse to either computing, blaming, distracting, or placating. Often a couple will be engaged in a lively way with difficult and newly discussed material, hit a pause, then one of them will suddenly start in one of those unproductive directions. It is crucial, when you spot that, to interrupt and take them back to the place where they were: "I noticed that your tone of voice changed right after that pause. You became very severe, and your wife cringed in her chair. Could you try saying what was on your mind then in a different way?" Generally it is best to let the conversation proceed, if the partner you have stopped follows the instruction. If either returns to an ineffective mode, you will need to stop again and talk specifically about that. But if they can stay on the track of the original discussion, that will be more productive.

The object of this therapist activity is for the clients to be able to have these conversations without your saying anything at all. When they can do that, you will find yourself listening and enjoying, but doing little else. When that stage has been reached, the work is ready to either move deeper or terminate, depending on their desires.

# CHAPTER SEVEN

# COMMUNICATION: THE SPECIFIC TECHNIQUES

The techniques we've just described are aimed at containing couples within a potentially decisive conversation, helping them stay with an issue until they resolve it. The progress of the counseling can often be mapped from one of these decisive issue-specific negotiations to the next.

But there is another kind of explicit teaching that goes on throughout the process, although not aimed directly at decisive, high-profile conversations. It is focused on the constant upgrading of a couple's communication skills, which goes on whether or not a crucial issue is on the floor and is central to the average expectable gratification of day-to-day life. These skills are not used every moment, but every couple needs to be able to use them without fail, when needed.

The counselor watches for these skills, and if the couple does not demonstrate them spontaneously, the counselor indicates their existence with a question, models them, and, if necessary, directly teaches them.

## Preparatory and Concurrent Instruction

The single most important of these skills is use of the "I message." An "I message" occurs when I take explicit, personal responsibility for my feeling, my wish, my thought, my fantasy. It starts with "I," continues with a verb and a direct object, so that the intent of the speaker is unmistakable, and the linkage of the statement and the speaker is unambiguous: "I want you to go to the store and buy a gallon of milk." This is particularly important for couples in which individuality is not clearly established, in which the spouses are fond of saying "we want" and "we feel," or in which the husband or wife comes from a family that made it dangerous or uncomfortable to have obvious individual wishes and ideas.

The objective is to reach a point where both partners can understand that the husband's experience, feelings, wishes, and ideas are inevitably different in some ways from the wife's experience, feelings, wishes, and ideas; and, if possible, can understand the nature and extent of those differences. Many couples, especially those from very tight-knit families and those in relatively new relationships, believe that there is something wrong if both spouses are not constantly wanting and feeling the same things. So they pretend that is the case and often feel threatened if it appears not to be, as though that meant something horrible was wrong with their marriage.

In other couples, a spouse will use either "we" statements or impersonal generalizations ("People always . . ." or "Of course you believe . . .") as a way of indirectly claiming power to define the other's experience. The therapist needs to interrupt that, especially early in treatment, and ask the speaker to say "I." If he or she insists on staying with the "we," then the other partner should be asked whether the "we" is accurate, if it represents that person's thoughts and wishes also. If either partner says something that appears to mean that he or she believes or feels something, but says it in some other way, stop and insist that the person claim it personally and individually. In the process you are teaching that marriage is a relationship of two different individuals, which has to find a way of dealing with, not hiding from, the differences.

The counselor should refuse to let the spouses fail to represent themselves, unless there is a very good reason for it. Every time one speaks for the other, ask the person spoken for to verify or correct the message. The purpose is to extinguish that behavior except when there is reason to be certain. It pays to let this pass only in very difficult marriages when it is not safe for one partner to openly disagree with the other. Usually you will be seeing such spouses separately, though occasionally there will be reason to have them together—usually to work on specifically delimited areas.

Another skill you will be routinely teaching is the balancing of conversations, making sure each member gets the air time needed to equally influence the outcome. One way to insure this is to ask for the other's response to every statement a speaker makes. This should not be a woodenly mechanical procedure, interrupting at every punctuation mark, but a dependable question from you every paragraph or two, inviting the one not talking to comment. This is another indirect way of teaching that marriage works better when there are two whole people, with all their inevitable differences. Many couples sound as though one member actually makes up 90 percent of the unit, because the other fails to get an oar in when the one spouse is defining their common reality. In order to train the relatively silent partner to find a voice and the highly verbal one to listen for it, your task is to interrupt the flow and make room for the one who won't speak.

Another important skill you need to practice and teach is that of clarifying incongruent or confusing messages. Any time a husband or wife says something that sounds important but you don't know what is meant, interrupt and ask. The odds are that the spouse doesn't know either, but is tired of doing the asking, or suspects the message is supposed to be understood. This applies both to verbal ambiguity and to messages that are confusing because the verbal and nonverbal messages conflict. When the words indicate delight with something the spouse did, but the way it is said sounds either bored or angry, that message has to be confusing to the spouse. Point out the inconsistency and ask how it should be taken. It isn't necessarily the case that the words are false and the nonverbals true, or vice versa, though that is a typical pattern.

Sometimes the verbal message is true in one way, or of one part of the speaker; and the nonverbals are true in a different way or of a different part of the speaker. The speaker is often unaware of the duality of the messages and the confusion they produce. One way to intervene is by asking, "Should I believe your words or your tone of voice?" or "What should I do with the difference between your words and your facial expression?" or "Were you aware that your tender, affirming words were countered by the snarl in your voice and your clenched fist?" Any of these interventions alert the speaker to the difficulty of translating the messages, and the hearer to the fact that he or she is not the only one having trouble doing it.

There is another important thing the counselor needs to be doing regularly, and teaching the clients to do, and that is to check out how accurately they are hearing and interpreting the conversation. This is a good thing to do when you don't know what else to do, because it gives both you and the clients a chance to review what you think has been going on, which often sparks a response from one of them or alerts you to a question you need to be considering.

"Checking out" is a process in which one party says to another, "This is what I think you just said. Do I have it right?" It provides the person being checked a chance to correct any misconceptions. It is important to check with one or both parties any time the counselor is confused, is uncertain what someone meant, or at important punctuation points in the conversation—such as when the counselor is about to change the subject or ask for a firm decision about something that's been discussed. The spouses need to check with each other whenever they are unsure they have grasped the other's intent, and need to have it perfectly clear so they can respond accurately. I make it a practice to summarize and check out my understandings of what spouses are saying to each other at least a couple of times a session. The timing of this is important. You don't want to interrupt a strongly flowing conversation, but a summary and checking out may be useful as the first stage of the next transition.

This is a vital tool for keeping errors from becoming established in either party's understanding. Don't allow anything to be laid down in the memory unless you or the partner has checked it out first.

Checking out is an important way to implement a belief the counselor should always be teaching: joint responsibility for the outcome of every conversation. Many people come into counseling believing that the confusion in the marriage is the spouse's fault, unaware that there is anything they can do to improve communication. The counselor's task includes helping both parties learn to keep conversations from being completely steered by one spouse. The person who checks out cannot say later that he or she did not understand what the other meant.

There are a number of techniques couples can use to activate the dual responsiblity for outcomes. Spouses can watch each other for signs of comprehension and agreement, and ask about it when those signs are absent. If one does not understand or believe something the other has said, he or she can say so and stick to it until something is said that is intelligible and believable. The fit between the partner's present emotional state and what the spouse would expect the partner to be feeling, given the events that have just transpired, can be compared. And if the fit doesn't feel right, the spouse can ask about it: "Usually when Mary asks to use your car, you resent it at least a little. Something seems to be different this time. What's up?"

Much of the failure to complete communication happens because the receivers of a message are shirking their responsibility to be sure they understand, or because the original sender ignores signs of confusion or disbelief on the part of the receivers. With all parties attending to the way the conversation is going, it's hard to foul it up.

The clients also need to learn to ask questions and to do it well. In a marriage that is working well, each has and uses the right to ask the other anything. That doesn't mean the other always must answer, but it's always O.K. to raise any question. An accompanying responsibility is that the questions be genuine requests for information, not attempts to browbeat or manipulate. So if partners rarely ask each other to fill in missing data, or almost all statements stand without requests for further elaboration, it is important to find ways to deepen and complexify the communication. Your questions to each of them will help model that. But ultimately it may be necessary to indicate your permission, even urge them to challenge and express their curiosity to each other. You might ask, "Is there anything you'd like to ask her about that?" or "Did you get all the information you'd like to have when she described the situation?" If that type of intervention does not produce increasing give and take, give them direct feedback about their unusual willingness to let what each one says stand at face value, their apparent lack of curiosity or willingness to engage.

Another vital process you should be teaching and modeling is the monitoring of the emotional level of the clients and the comparison between a certain level and what the circumstances seem to dictate. For any given topic, we need some idea about how high the stakes will be if the couple brings it up. When it does appear, if the talk is at the emotional pitch we expected, our understanding of the people is confirmed. But if the stakes are much higher or much lower than we expected, it means something was flawed in our picture of the clients; and that something needs to be identified and corrected. "I knew this subject would be a little tense, but I didn't expect the feelings to be this strong. Where's all the energy coming from?" is one way to pursue this kind of clarification. Another would be to ask, "Do either of you know why this topic causes so much feeling?" A third option: "I must have misunderstood something. I thought this question would be almost impossible to talk about. Can you tell me how you're managing it so well?"

These counselor habits need to be built in so firmly that they are produced automatically. They go one step beyond setting up the counselor's communicative world and begin to directly teach a way of being with each other that uses speech to share information and respect. They lead toward the ability to talk skillfully about the decisive issues of life and provide the flexibility and ease that will serve the couple happily after they have settled the major conflicts that brought them into counseling.

## Modular Teachings—For Recurrent Problems

Some couples catch on very slowly. Stubborn resistance, impoverished backgrounds, rigid attitudes, or lack of intelligence make it difficult to learn new skills and discuss significant issues at the same time. For such people, it is occasionally necessary to put aside discussion of the issues, keep the subject matter simple and nonthreatening, and spend time teaching very basic skills.

Several modules, self-contained brief experiences designed to build a particular piece of conversational ability, have been developed. One of the simplest of these is designed for couples that have trouble getting the verbal message straight from one partner to the other. Often this happens in highly competitive marriages, when one partner is already constructing the next response before the other finishes speaking, and so does not hear. The remedy is a *paraphrasing* exercise, more an attempt to condition a new habit than to add a skill. The counselor declares that for a few minutes, the rules of the session will be changed: After one partner speaks, the other is not allowed to respond to the content without first paraphrasing the statement and getting the spouse's agreement that the other has it right. Once that is done, a response is allowed. The counselor has to be quite active at first with interruptions and refocusing to make this technique useful, since people who need it rarely fall into it easily. But usually within five or ten minutes the counselor will have made the point that speaking without really hearing the other will not be accepted, and it will be safe to return to a freer discussion. The couple knows the counselor always has the option of going back to the exercise if the competition gets out of hand.

Another important tactic is the eliciting of *operational definitions* for a couple's "buzz words" about relationships. This is a gambit developed and mentioned to me by George Siskind, an Indianapolis psychologist who believes that people often fail to understand what others are really saying when they use fashionable words for behavior. He contends that when one partner says the other should be more sensitive, or more forgiving, or understanding, or accepting, a great deal of wasted effort and painful confusion often develop because the other tries in the wrong direction. With spouses who couch their demands in such global terms, Siskind recommends a two-step process. Once the word being worked on is identified, he asks the partner who is being asked for that behavior to say what he or she thinks the partner means. When that person gives a definition, Siskind asks the partner (the one who originally asked for the commodity) if the other has it right. If so, fine; if not, how not? That process continues until the one who is being asked to produce the behavior produces a definition that satisfies the asker. Then comes the second step, in which the askee is to describe a situation in which the quality in question is present, repeating the description until the person who has identified the quality says it is right. Then the counseling can proceed with a reasonable expectation that everyone knows what is being talked about.

Let's say the wife has said she wants the husband to be more accepting of her. The counselor's task is to have the husband say what he thinks she means: "Bill, can you tell Sally how you think she defines accepting?" Bill attempts to do that, and the counselor asks Sally, "Did he get it exactly right?" If she says no, she must say how, and Bill must redefine the word until she gives her O.K. When she does, the counselor says to Bill, "Now I want you to describe a situation in which someone has been accepting, as Sally would see it." Bill describes a situation, and the counselor asks Sally if that is what she would call accepting. If not, she provides more data, and Bill tries again until there is agreement that he understands what she means. This does not mean that Bill is necessarily agreeing to do what Sally asks. It does mean that until Bill understands her request, nothing else can happen.

Another difficulty occasionally calls for modular learning: when spouses seem unable to sense each other's feeling responses to situations or are unaccustomed to talking about their own feeling responses. A useful tool for that situation is an experience sometimes called *empathy training*. The rule change from ordinary conversation is a simple one: after each statement, the partners are asked to say what each thinks the other is feeling, and how it has changed since the previous inquiry. Often this reveals the partners have given little attention to how either is feeling. It also can help you discover whether there are particular feelings that each is blind to in the other, or in themselves. When that is true, there is always a reason, and finding it can greatly enhance the work.

A more elaborate way of getting at the same problem has been developed by Beryl Chernick and Avinoam Chernick, Canadian physicians who have specialized in sex therapy (*In Touch: Putting Sex Back into Love and Marriage*, Macmillan of Canada, 1977). Their technique involves the use of *neutral pictures*, which spouses or therapist can clip out of whatever magazines are handy. The Chernicks concluded that most couples have sexual problems because the partners don't share feelings well, and they have developed this technique to further that process in a nonthreatening way. It begins with the counselor selecting a picture and presenting it first to one spouse, then to the other. The spouses simply report what feeling it arouses in them. At first, the only allowable response is "I feel _____ in response to that picture." Once those feelings have been reported, they are asked to say why they think that picture produced that particular feeling. Neither is allowed to criticize the other for having a particular feeling. The counselor begins this experience with pictures that are quite impersonal or feeling-distant—inanimate objects, sunsets, nature scenes. After the couple has become more able to talk about emotions, the counselor can introduce scenes of human intimacy and anger. This module lends itself to the assigning of homework, since after the spouses have developed some minimal competence at staying with the task, they can spend time with it at home, each selecting a certain number of pictures.

This technique is good for helping partners experience sharing of feelings as data about their inner lives, rather than as demand or manipulation. The hearer does nothing but take in the information about the feelings of the other. These instructions free both from any need to change their feelings.

Another set of modules has been developed to help couples learn to profit from anger and aggression. Yetta Bernhard and Barbara Wyden compiled several of these in *Aggression Lab* (Kendall/Hunt, 1971), and George Bach and Peter Wyden recount others in *The Intimate Enemy* (Avon Books, 1968). Perhaps the most powerful of these techniques is titled "Fair Fight for Change," and bears a strong resemblance to a stylized version of conjoint counseling. It is especially useful when a couple has acknowledged that a particular issue must be resolved. In the original version, at least two coaches are used, but one counselor can fill both roles if necessary. One spouse is asking for a specific change, and the first part of the exercise is between that spouse and the coach or counselor. In this step, that spouse, working with the coach, refines the request so that it is clear and specific. Once that is done, the request is presented to the partner. The counselor then asks the first spouse if it was presented satisfactorily. If so, that part is completed.

Then the coach/counselor turns his or her attention to the receiving spouse, first finding out if that partner is completely clear about what is being asked. If not, the counselor helps the person frame questions to further clarify the request. Then the counselor helps the receiver come to a clear statement in regard to the request. Three responses are permitted: yes, no, or a counterproposal. The latter is the most common, and the counselor works with the receiver to frame the response in the same clear and precise way the request was framed. That is presented to the first spouse, with the counselor again functioning as the gatekeeper who helps clarify the language of the proposal. The process continues until one partner offers a counterproposal that the other accepts, with the counselor alternating attention, clarifying the wording of proposals, making sure they are clearly understood, and helping both partners examine their feelings about the proposal they have heard.

There is a huge repertoire of such teaching modules available from the literature on assertiveness training, marriage enrichment, human relations training, and organizational development. These modules are useful ways for some people to learn, and are almost entirely capable of being modified for standard conjoint work.

## Who These Methods Will Help—And How Much

Almost every couple will be helped to some extent through the methods discussed in this chapter, but there is a large minority that will need more complex tools—and a small minority that won't be touched. The majority of counselees will find new resources which they can use to develop new behaviors and construct new and more viable dreams. Spouses will find that the ability to talk more discriminatingly about a wider range of their experience equips them to design what they need in the way of new patterns of relationship to each other.

There will be a small percentage of couples, however, in which the relationship gets worse as communication gets better. Usually these are people who are locked into a highly reactive, competitive, often long-standing marriage— twenty-five years of holy deadlock. In such couples, with each spouse knowing precisely what goes on inside the other, each is only given more ammunition with which to cause pain; and the deeply entrenched horror of being controlled makes it all but impossible for either to respond to the other's direct requests for assistance.

Such couples drive counselors crazy, since standard methods do not work. The more the spouses know about each other, the worse they fight. This kind of couple stimulated the creation of a new school of marital and family therapy, variously termed *strategic* or *paradoxical*. It operates on the principle that counselors should keep secret what they actually want a couple to do, thereby providing the spouses nothing to react against. It capitalizes on the intense oppositionalism of such couples by prescribing the symptoms ("Why don't you see how much you can punish each other for the rest of this hour?"), giving paradoxical injunctions, setting up double-binds, and reframing things with a distinct tongue-in-cheek flavor.

This kind of therapy works very well with a wide range of couples, but is difficult to use when the counselors have multiple roles and relationships with the recipients. It requires that counselors say outrageous things which are both helpful and confusing. Since pastors and other frontline people helpers often need to say exactly what they mean, the introduction of this added complexity is often unacceptable. However, therapists who do use these tools now practice in most communities and would be happy to have these referrals—couples who are almost impossible to deal with in a parish situation.

Another group will be helped, but not enough, by the previously described communication methods. Such spouses will learn to communicate better, but will retreat from doing so because they don't want too much intimacy; or they will communicate better, but manage to do so without removing the complaints that brought them for counseling in the first place.

Such people will not get worse when you get them to talk to each other, but their failure to improve will be marked by repeated returns to patterns that have made them miserable before. It's as though they get a reward from their pain, or from the repetition of the familiar patterns, which counts for more than the tension and conflict those patterns produce. So even when they experience feeling better in the sessions, they don't repeat the decisive behaviors outside.

Another variation of this style is the couple in which a spouse repeatedly misunderstands the intentions and motives of the other, or at least pretends to. In response to such misunderstandings, one or both will invest so much energy in self-protection that no energy is left for relating productively. This pattern often seems impervious to the communication-based model we've been discussing, which may succeed in moving them from one point to another along their accustomed cycle, but will not move them out of that cycle into freer ways of dealing with each other.

These couples require a method aimed at producing individual personality change as well as marital growth, and often need to be in a helping relationship for many months or even a few years. The time requirements make it impractical for most pastors to counsel them, and successful management of the individual personality variables requires additional training as well. Productive work with these people falls on the therapy side of the counseling-therapy border, and requires a major commitment of time in learning the skills.

There is no reason pastors can't learn these techniques, if they want to make the necessary investment of up to four years of additional training. That is often the motivation and hunger that lead clergy toward specialized pastoral counseling training. But clergy who do not develop their abilities in this direction need to understand what happens in such therapy, so they can prepare people they are referring with some knowledge of what to expect. An outline and rationale for this more interpretive and deep-reaching process is presented in chapter 9.

# SEXUAL COUNSELING IN THE PASTORAL CONTEXT

Though sex is more a sorrow than a joy to many of the couples who come to us for counseling, they usually don't present it as the main thing they want to remedy. The public suspicion that clergy do not know much about sex has something to do with that, but the larger reason is that parishioners have a public relationship with their pastor, making embarrassment more of a problem than it would be in a totally private relationship. The public nature of ministry also makes it unusual and perhaps unwise for a pastor to make sexual counseling a widely known specialty. It may invite suspicion you don't need.

But a pastor does need competence in both understanding and intervening in sexual problems. A clear, if not detailed awareness of normal and abnormal sexual function is crucial to marriage counseling, since sexual issues interpenetrate so much marital distress. Most sexual problems are caused by prior relationship failures, but once a sexual difficulty is entrenched, it becomes a major obstacle to a satisfying marriage.

There are three major types of sexual difficulties that will typically come to a pastor's attention, corresponding to the stages of marriage: very early marriage, where ignorance is often a problem; mid-marriage, where the difficulty is almost always situational; and mature marriage, which often contains deeply entrenched and long-standing sexual impasses.

## Sex as an Early Marriage Crisis

Many couples find the honeymoon a sexual nightmare from which they never recover. Expectations are very high, especially for couples that have not been sexually active before marriage; romantic fantasy makes a jubilant sexual beginning terribly important, and a sense of humor hard to come by. It is not unusual in their early sexual encounters for couples to discover some characteristics or preferences that are frightening, repulsive, or unacceptably embarrassing.

Many sexually inexperienced couples will be surprised to discover that they have hitherto unknown attitudes toward being touched or seen, or that their partners do. When these early discoveries are combined with intense pressure to succeed, it is sometimes excruciatingly difficult to talk about the new and troubling discovery. If not talked about, or if talking about them frightens or humiliates either party, the experience can become a total barrier to sexual intimacy. This often produces sexual avoidance that weakens a marriage for life. If either partner has feelings of vulnerability about her or his own attractiveness or desirability (and which of us does not?), these can be made much worse by even small disappointments with honeymoon sex. And if either has strong feelings of responsibility to be competent in this area, and discovers that he or she is not, the potential for relationship-crippling shame is redoubled.

Though early sexual disappointment is extremely dangerous to a marriage, such crises are amenable to prompt, decisive interventions with basically the same communication focus we have already discussed. No specialized knowledge of sexual dysfunction is required to make a marriage-saving difference, and there are a number of points at which crucial moves can be made.

This is one of the areas in which a pastor's premarital counseling can be particularly important. Plant the thought that some people do not get their sexual relationship right in the first few weeks of marriage, even if they have been sexually happy together during the courtship. The emotional climate changes when the "I do's" are said, and it is not unusual for a sexual relationship that has been enjoyable and untroubled to flounder in a sea of familial predictability, fears of commitment and entrapment, and oedipal apprehension. If couples are reminded that those first few weeks frequently are anxious and unpredictable, it can take some of the embarrassed sense of failure out of things not being perfect. Another important word to leave with couples before the ceremony: If they do have difficulty in this area, it is very important that they seek help promptly and not let the awkwardness or pain of their early sexual meetings become the norm for the marriage. Sexual pain can become entrenched early, especially when self-consciousness is high, and it is important to reverse it before it solidifies.

Another valuable move the pastor can make—one that is not available to the office therapist—is to drop by a few months after the marriage for a little preventive maintenance. The purposes of such a visit include listening for signs of trouble, normalizing the typical newlywed isolation (letting them know you understand if they are not getting to church as often as they might—some things are more important), providing a link to the congregation through your person, and saying some things again, in case they didn't sink in during the premarital time (a time when precious little does sink in). It can be useful to tell them that the first six months are the hardest part of marriage for many couples, and especially useful to listen for their response to that. If there is more than a flicker of recognition, stay with it. Though for fortunate couples, sexual pleasure makes up for the difficult transitions of those months, it is important for the pastor to remember that it does not always work that way, and to let them know you know it, especially if they have given a hint that things aren't all rosy. If that leads to a conversation about the problem, you can handle it like a standard counseling interview.

Any time a newly married couple makes a request for pastoral attention, be alert for sexual problems. It is important not to assume that couples will lead with these concerns, since those most likely to have them are those who have the most difficulty talking about them. If a couple is expressing any dissatisfaction with each other or the new relationship, ask how sex is going.

Once you have asked, do not be satisfied with anything less than an answer. If a new couple is having trouble in this part of life, the partners are going to be very frightened and/or ashamed. There will be a tendency to half-say things, to try to avoid hurting each other and embarrassing themselves or you. Since these early sexual problems are most often the result of difficulty in expressing preferences and registering satisfactions or dissatisfactions, it is predictable that they may not tell you about the trouble directly. Your contribution can be to help them speak about the things they have been unable to speak about.

What needs to happen is the upgrading of their overall communication skills, and the application of these to talk about their sex life. Almost all such newlywed sexual problems can be cured by conversation, the rare exceptions being persons who have major psychological problems. But the curative conversations are ones such a couple does not know how to have.

There are standard areas of needed conversation you need to be alert to. One of the most important is frequency, which partners will sometimes disagree about while being unwilling to reveal the disagreement. So the spouse wanting less will provide more, all the while building up a silent resentment that erodes the quality and enjoyment of sex for both of them. If they don't say anything about frequency, while indicating that there is some problem with sex, ask about it.

Another typical problem area is unexpressed dissatisfaction with the other's sexual technique or willingness to experiment. If these people, like many newlyweds, protect each other's feelings at their own expense, you can perform an important service by asking each of them to tell the other directly what they do and don't like about the way he or she makes love. If the issue is not addressed, you can ask if both are regularly achieving orgasm, and if not, why not. What is interfering? Ask what they have learned about each other's signals in sexual situations and help each check out with the partner whether they are reading the other correctly. Generally, you can help them speak their dissatisfactions and talk about new behaviors that would help, without having to be a sexual wizard yourself. Both of them know what they want and are not getting, and saying this in a way that is not damning is often all that is required.

Another good area to explore whenever there is indication of a sexual problem is each partner's satisfaction with the other's overall attitude toward sex, especially as shown in comfort with nudity, preference for talk or noise during sex, and intensity of physical contact itself. Often one partner will label a difference between them as meaning something other than what it means, and a frank exploratory conversation about such meanings can remove much misunderstanding. Not all differences can be removed by talking, but it rarely makes any of these problems worse, and it usually helps to identify points of possible compromise and clarify each person's motivation.

I cannot say strongly enough that fairly small, simple interventions in the first weeks or months of marriage can be very powerful. Sexual dissatisfaction can become institutionalized quickly at the beginning of marriage and is a terribly difficult obstacle to marital happiness. Thirty minutes or an hour in those first few weeks can pay dividends for a couple's lifetime, and their omission can extract a heavy price.

### Sex as a Mid-Marriage Dysfunction

The second variety of sexual problem occurs primarily in couples that have not had the early uncertainty and pain we have just discussed. These couples have been married anywhere from a few months to twenty years and have almost always had periods of happy and satisfying sex together before the onset of the problems that led them to seek a counselor.

Their complaints are primarily and explicitly sexual. Couples report them as starting at a particular time, not as having been chronic throughout the relationship. They take a form different from the conscious fear and pain of early marriage. These couples report that something is interfering with their sexual adjustment now that hadn't been troubling before, and it seems to be something outside their control. They complain most often of a man's impotence or premature ejaculation, of inability of either spouse to reach orgasm, of marked differences in desire between the spouses, and of vaginal constriction in the woman.

These difficulties are almost always situational in origin, with only a few of the causative situations being sexual. The single most important mechanism that produces such sexual dysfunction is suppressed anger, which usually arises from a failed expectation outside the sexual sphere. So when a couple reports a sexual problem in the course of a marriage that usually has been sexually satisfying, the first thing to look for is the possibility that one of the spouses is angry at the other and isn't saying anything about it. The task there, of course, is to locate the source of the anger, the situation out of which it has come, and do whatever is necessary to change it. Then the anger usually goes away, and with it the sexual dysfunction.

A marked change in life situation will often throw a couple into this kind of difficulty. You will find that the sexual problem started within a few weeks or months of an upheaval such as a job change for one of the spouses, a change in parental responsibilities or patterns, a physical change in one partner—illness, pregnancy, amputation, weight gain or loss—or a major shift in the extended family network of one of the spouses. The death or divorce of parents or a sibling's geographical move can cause a change in a couple's contract which, if not thoroughly negotiated, can leave one partner feeling shortchanged and angry.

Spouses who develop a sexual dysfunction usually have responded to the situational change by attempting to keep on doing things the way they had been doing them. They either will not have noticed the severity of the change, or one will have tried to protect the other by trying to absorb all the added stress. After a time, continuing the old patterns in a new situation will produce injustices in the marriage—one partner will be getting more satisfaction, or less inconvenience, than the other. They may keep quiet about it, feeling it would be unjust to complain. For a time, this martyrdom may work; but after the imbalance reaches a given point, the enthusiasm of the disadvantaged spouse for events that please the partner will ebb. Sexual desire may diminish, and potency along with it. Or a woman may have trouble becoming aroused, or may not feel motivated to seek orgasm. If those signs are not noticed and the causes sought out, sexual avoidance that can lastingly impair closeness can develop.

This is usually the point at which spouses seek help. The most helpful thing the counselor can do is to help them locate the life changes that disrupted the sexual relationship. You can begin by asking for a thorough recounting of the major events in both their lives and their extended family's lives in the weeks or months before the trouble began. Often you will find a major shift that the relationship hasn't digested. It produced a new balance between them. Once you have understood the nature of that new balance, ask about the meanings of sex under these new conditions. You will often hear something about sex seeming to ratify a way of organizing life in this new situation, which one partner doesn't wish to ratify, but hasn't said much about. That partner has just cooled toward the other.

Once that point has been identified, it is a relatively simple matter to start negotiating ways to restore the marital balance. Getting their sexual lives back on the right track is typically such a strong motivator that spouses are eager to cooperate with each other. Once the willingness is recognized, the anger level often drops so that sexual interest and ability returns, even if the solution to the situational problem has not yet been found. Experiencing the other's willingness to help look for a solution is often enough; though, of course, a solution will eventually have to be found for the improvement to hold.

In a fairly small percentage of cases, this process will not be enough to restore happy sexual sharing. Either you won't find a situational imbalance in the couple's recent history, or you will find it, successfully negotiate the change in handling it, but the sexual problem won't go away. Then you have a full-fledged sexual dysfunction on your hands, in which the couple has learned a sexually deadening pattern that they are unconsciously reinforcing.

Such symptoms begin in particular instances of sexual failure and are perpetuated by the spouses' anxiety that the failure will be repeated. The original failure can come from any cause: anger at each other about something nonsexual, fatigue, intoxication, fear, or practically anything that interferes with sexual pleasure. Most couples have some unsatisfying sexual experiences at times, but couples that become dysfunctional compound them into chronic symptoms by being frightened at those original failures and worrying about them in subsequent sexual situations. That worry, coupled with the unspoken demand that the failure not be repeated, raises anxiety and interferes with the spouses' ability to focus attention on pleasing themselves. That increases the probability that the failure will be repeated, and with each new failure the fear increases. The couple learns to expect failure, which increases the likelihood of sexual avoidance and/or repetition of the dysfunction.

Because these are learned and reinforced behaviors, they are quite amenable to deconditioning, unlearning. Premature ejaculation is curable in over 95 percent of cases, and the other dysfunctions are successfully treated at almost as high a rate, if a couple has been sexually successful before the onset of this symptom. The pioneering work of William Masters and Virginia Johnson created much of the basic knowledge on which sex therapy techniques were built (*Human Sexual Inadequacy*, Little, Brown & Co., 1970); their own work in St. Louis, Helen Singer Kaplan's in New York (*The New Sex Therapy*, Brunner-Mazel, 1974), the Chernicks' in Toronto, and William Hartman and Marilyn Fythian's in California (*Treatment of Sexual Dysfunction*, Center for Marital and Sexual Studies, 1972), have produced a wealth of techniques that are as consistently successful as anything in the mental health field.

These techniques are not particularly difficult to learn, but most pastors don't find it advantageous to be identified as the sex therapy experts in their neighborhood. It is to your advantage, though, to know enough about the practices and techniques so you can let people you are referring know what to expect. There is a lot of public skepticism about sex therapy, and occasional frank exploitation within the field, so your education of those you refer can be valuable for them. In addition to the material presented here, it would be valuable to contact sex therapists in your area so you will know how they operate, making the information you pass on to parishioners that much more specific.

Many, though not all, sex therapists work in male-female teams. They believe that people are more willing to talk about sexual experience with members of their own sex, having less need to impress and less expectation of vulnerability. Furthermore, it helps to have trained persons present who experience sexuality from both sides of the gender boundary, so that an opposite-sex person who is not tainted by whatever anger or distrust lives in the marriage can speak for the sexual experience of that gender: "As a woman, it's this way for me . . . ."

One of the most important advantages of this arrangement is that it allows the therapists to model a man-woman relationship in which sex is discussed. If one of your couple does not expect men to ever listen to anything, then it is important for her to see that the male therapist listens to his colleague. If the man has never felt it possible to discuss such things with women present, it is valuable for him to see the therapists discuss them across gender boundaries. It's also useful for people who believe that talking about sex with an opposite-sex person is always an attempt at seduction to have a same-sex person in the room to transmit information and hear their experience while providing a safeguard against that seduction.

Most sex therapy teams take a careful, extended, sexual history. If it is a male-female team, the man will work with the man, the woman with the woman. They give particular attention to the point where the spouses first became aware of sexual differences, how they became aware, how they first experienced sexual feelings, how they felt toward their own sexual parts and bodies in general, and how they first began presexual and sexual contact with other persons. Therapists spend a lot of time tracing the development of sexual intensity in the spouses' early relationships, paying special attention to points of unusual discomfort as well as points of high arousal. They try to get a feel for what labels a situation as sexually exciting for the person, as well as the elements that define a situation as sexually impossible. In the process they are subtly teaching that sexual behavior is learned and that this development of repertoire and inhibition follows much the same steps as the learning of other complex human processes. By the time the history taking is finished, both therapists should know the way the current symptom fits with the past sexual lives of both partners—whether the overtly symptomatic person has had this problem before, and in what situations; and whether the partner has ever been with anyone who had this problem before, and how he or she felt about it and reacted to it. This material can be shared between the spouses or not, depending on whether it involves secrets that would cause further difficulty if exposed.

The first step following the history is usually a session that outlines the different steps in the process and prescribes a time-limited period of sexual abstinence. This is a very important, though not instantly popular prescription. The therapist will usually ask the couple to avoid all explicitly sexual contact, no touching of genitals, for at least a week and sometimes longer.

There is a reason for this. Sexual behavior, both successful and unsuccessful, is learned. The spouses have typically had a period of satisfying sex, often many years without trouble, then have fairly recently encountered the inability to gratify each other. The more thoroughly the therapy can disrupt the process by which the newly established symptom has been learned and reinforced, the greater the likelihood that the older, successful, more deeply established pattern will reemerge. Further, it is very important to remove the pressure to perform. By the time the average couple has presented for sex therapy, the spouses are so frightened of having sex that the fear is the major factor in the failures. By telling them they can't have sex for a time, you remove the situation that produces the greatest discomfort, and do not point the finger of guilt at the person with the obvious symptom.

After a period of abstinence has calmed things down a bit, sex therapists usually prescribe a gradually intensifying series of sensate-focus exercises. They will instruct the partners to spend a specified period of time—beginning with a brief period (20 to 30 minutes)—giving each other physical pleasure that is specifically not sexual. A combination of massage and caress is recommended, with clear instructions to avoid the typical erogenous zones, and with further instructions that the partners talk about the experience while they are doing it. They are to let each other know what feels good, what not so good; what is pleasant to do and not so pleasant. There are at least three reasons this assignment is important: (1) Following the period of abstinence, all their sexual habits are somewhat more flexible than they had been when the symptom was being repeated regularly, so you have a chance to influence foreplay behaviors positively, building good habits; (2) These couples often have not well understood the continuum between sensual and sexual touching and need an experience of building sexual excitement and affectional feelings through touches that are not defined as sexual; (3) The partners typically have not talked much or well about what they liked and didn't like about physical contact, so this teaches a communication style they will need as they get into more specific sexual touching later in the process.

The steps up to this point are pretty much the same with any sexual dysfunction. Once the partners have demonstrated in the sensate-focus exercise that they can give each other physical pleasure and have shown that they can use conversation to improve the quality of both the pleasure and the relationship, they are ready for exercises specific to their symptoms. The best developed techniques are used with male impotence and premature ejaculation, and for vaginismus (vaginal constriction) in the female. In the two male-visible disorders, the techniques are similar. Both involve the couple in bringing the male to the point of either full erection or near-orgasm, then backing off, cooling down, and starting over. The point is to prove to both the man and the woman that if an erection is lost, it can be readily regained; and/or that if orgasm is sensed as approaching, it can be delayed and the process restarted. Men are taught to recognize the point of ejaculatory inevitability and decrease the stimulation to delay the orgasm. The woman needs to be a part of that process so she can understand why it matters that she cooperate. Both are also taught what produces and discourages erections in this particular male, and how quickly he can get a new one, once an old one has passed away. With those two learnings well established, the fear of sexual failure diminishes rapidly for both partners, and with the passing of the fear, the symptom usually passes as well.

All the sexual manipulation is done by a couple in the privacy of the home, reporting back to the therapists on the successes and failures. The latter make suggestions, alter the exercises, and take responsibility for regulating the couple's return to unencumbered sexual activity.

Vaginismus is a simpler clinical problem, sometimes treated with the woman alone. The standard treatment is a combination of relaxation techniques and the insertion of a series of size-graded cones into the vagina, the size of the cone being increased as the relaxation creates a larger opening. If the woman has a partner who wants to be involved in the process, that can be helpful, but the disorder is treatable without one.

Most sex therapists regard sexual dysfunction as a couple problem, requiring an alteration in the couple's system to produce cure. The original failure is often a response to a relational impasse, and the attitude of the apparently nonsymptomatic spouse can often be a large factor in maintaining the symptom. Hence cure will happen only if both spouses want it and are willing to make their behavior available for scrutiny and change. On the other hand, such therapists usually see an individual's sexual satisfaction as that person's own responsibility. Each needs to guide the relationship and its sexual expressions so that her or his own needs are met, and attempt to respond to the other's cues in ways that enable the other's needs to be met as well. But no one can force another person to have an orgasm or an erection, hence each partner needs to be paying primary attention to what he or she needs for satisfaction, at the same time listening to cues about what the other needs.

One of the most controversial and titillating aspects of sex therapy has been the use of sexual surrogates. Couples will have heard about that, and some are frightened of sex therapy altogether because of it. Pastors need to know enough about this practice to reassure or encourage potential referrals. Surrogates are almost never used if a committed partner is available, but only as a last resort when a person who lacks a continuing partner needs to learn to be sexual with someone who will make that as easy as possible. They are never used without the full awareness and agreement of the client and, I repeat, almost never with married persons. On the other hand, they are used occasionally by reputable and competent sex therapists and do perform a valuable service, especially with persons who have been socially isolated and are sexually inept. Obviously, a pastor might wish to know whether a therapist who is being considered uses surrogates, and on what basis.

Another important feature of sex therapy is that it is usually brief. The typical length of treatment for impotence, premature ejaculation, or vaginismus, in couples that previously have had good sexual adjustment, is under ten sessions. If a couple does not have a major relationship problem, and the partners have previously demonstrated the ability to enjoy each other sexually, this process is a speedy adjustment, a prompt deprogramming of a destructive habit, and should not become a lengthy relationship.

If an individual or a couple has never been sexually successful, the problems are very different. Sex therapy is sometimes indicated in such cases, but the kind required for these primary sexual dysfunctions is more similar to psychotherapy. It can last a long time and is one of the more difficult and exciting tasks in the entire therapeutic spectrum.

## Sex as a Continuing Catastrophe

Occasionally the counselor will run into couples who have been married twenty years or more, and sex has always been bad. They had a miserable honeymoon, and things have been getting worse since. Sex will have all but disappeared from their lives, with frequency falling off to once a month or less and remaining at that level for years.

Such couples do not usually complain about their sexual problems. They have gotten used to not having sex often or enjoyably, so some other difficulty will be required for them to seek help. And they usually do have other difficulties. Theirs are multiproblem marriages, marked by parallel lives, poor and infrequent communication, triangulation (with children, jobs, or lovers), and often substance abuse or chronic physical illness.

Most often one of these problems will bring such couples to a counselor. As the counselor explores the parameters of that token problem, the poverty of the relationship and the massiveness of the obstacles will gradually reveal themselves. Couples in that situation often test a counselor by confessing only a discrete segment of their pain, hoping against hope that the counselor will find the rest and offer a remedy. In fact, such spouses will often have decided many years earlier that life wasn't going to hold much satisfaction for them. Only occasionally, when something disturbs the resignation, will they muster some energy to see if the deadlock can be loosened.

Though such couples typically have massive sexual problems, careful evaluation is required before making a decision to work on them. For most of these marriages, the sudden development of an enjoyable sexual relationship would fit so poorly with the rest of the traffic between the couple that it would quickly be drowned by the pain of poor communication, mutual hostility and suspicion, and other preoccupations and commitments. Only when those difficulties have been diminished should sex therapy be attempted. When these obstacles are ignored and such an attempt made, it is often possible to produce more physical closeness, and even sexual frequency, for a short time. But the greater physical proximity and increased time together, without a corresponding increase in emotional sensitivity or mutual respect, only puts them in a better position (closer) to wound each other. The resulting increase in distrust and their disappointment in the therapy's results typically build greater barriers than were previously present.

Lengthy and unsatisfying marriages are very difficult for any counseling intervention. The spouses typically have deep individual pathology. Their communication can usually be improved, but improving it does not often improve the relationship. The problem often is that they communicate their mutual distaste and indifference all too well. Improved communication will leave them as great sources of pain for each other as they were previously.

Successful intervention with these long-standing miserable marriages requires an intense therapeutic investment. There are three major approaches: (1) a more interpretive mode of marital therapy, which takes as its goals both individual personality change and preservation/enrichment of the marriage; (2) individual psychotherapy for one or both partners, lasting anywhere from two to five years, or even longer; and (3) paradoxical or strategic therapy, which is readily learnable but typically involves major conflicts for pastors and other professionals with a public role. Furthermore, there are strong disagreements within the professional community as to whether the changes produced will be lasting for such couples.

An enjoyable sexual life is commonly thought indispensable for a lasting and gratifying marriage, and the counselor should be alert to opportunities to help a couple move in that direction. Early marriage crises can reveal major attitudinal barriers and will respond well to minimal interventions; mid-marriage crises are usually situational and respond successfully to sex therapy techniques; and older, entrenched marriages which have never been sexually happy require attack on a wide front, with all the therapeutic power the counselor and his referral network can muster.

# CHAPTER NINE

# *I*NTERPRETATION: SPEAKING THE TRUTH IN LOVE

*S*ome couples will not be helped enough by the communication-centered approach we have laid out. Spouses will improve their skills at talking to each other, but find that their unhappiness stays about the same, or even becomes worse. Other couples will improve those skills for a time, but the resulting truthful conversations will lead spouses to discover enough unpleasant things in each other that they won't want to be closer. Still others become better, but discover in the process that there are repeated cycles within their relationship that drag it back down. The communication-based approach by itself will not change them, so something else is needed.

The problem these couples have is that the original dream contained a flaw, a contradiction between the apparent dream and a hidden vision held by one or both members. One or both (usually both) have a very strong longing for things that either are not in the shared and agreed-upon dream, or that directly contradict it. The improvement in communication helps them obtain more of the things in the shared dream, but it does not do much to bring those other wishes into the open and find out how they can be integrated or, if necessary, renounced. And those wishes, if ungratified, keep their bearers unhappy, despite their achievement of the agreed-upon goals of the marriage; and in their attempt to be gratified, they will produce feelings and behavior that disrupt all attempts to reach the objectives of the public dream.

## Mate Selection and the Transferential Cycle

In couples who cannot profit from straightforward communication-based counseling, the mysteries of the courtship process have usually produced a pairing straight out of the decisive personnel patterns of childhood. Both will have chosen someone with major characteristics almost identical to those of a parent or, occasionally, someone with opposite traits.

The history taking early in counseling will have alerted you to this possibility, and the failure of a couple to achieve or maintain improvement will clinch the decision that a more interpretive approach is necessary.

The foundation for this marital deadlock is laid down early. As children we all must come to grips with a dominant parent, the one whose attitudes and actions have the most powerful impact on our day-to-day satisfaction. For years our well-being depends on the extent to which we gain the rewards this person has to offer, be those approval or stimulation or instruction or respect or merely freedom from punishment. We learn what it takes to get those rewards, if anything will get them; and we usually try to follow what we learn (unless we are so angry we decide it isn't worth the effort).

Most children develop a set of modestly reliable and gradually improving techniques for these purposes, and as they mature, they largely outgrow the need. The power to bestow the rewards builds up inside themselves over the years, and they are less and less dependent on the parent, or someone like him or her, to provide the good feelings at the center of life. But in the process, they do become skilled at getting those things from that kind of person, and in later life, they often choose to surround themselves with persons of that ilk so they can keep doing those things and getting the rewards. Life works fairly well that way, though it may be narrow and unadventurous.

The real difficulties develop when children fail to grow the needed skill at getting what the parent has to offer, or when they never figure out what it is the parent has, or when the parent does not have much to give. In such cases (which are very widespread) children have the longing but never learn a dependable method of meeting it. They occasionally push the right button, but the parent comes through with the reward only one out of five times, and they never know when they are going to lose. So the confidence in getting needs met does not develop, and a belief persists that there is a way to get them met if it is done exactly right—as it was done that time five tries ago when it worked. Further, these children's internal ability to reward themselves does not develop, so an external person is still needed to provide the growing or grown children with the feelings they want.

Children who have grown up in this situation arrive in adulthood with major difficulties. They are not very satisfied with life in general, since they typically don't get the responses they want from the world. They do not have much confidence in their skill at getting them, which undermines confidence in most of their other attributes. Further, they have identified a type of person as able to give those magical rewards—typically someone who shares major characteristics with the dominant parent—but have developed a seriously flawed method for getting them, even if they should find such a source. And they have an irresistible urge to try to get those responses, so their outlook on the world is dominated by scanning for a source of what they think they need. Their frustration over not having gotten enough of it remains open and demanding, and it doesn't let them rest until they find someone who appears to be able and willing to meet the need.

That frustration and the searching it creates provide the basis for transference—experiencing in a new relationship the feelings, perceptions, and attitudes that were originally felt, but not finished, in an old one. They continue to seek resolution through substitutes in the present.

Many people choose transference objects as mates, and a disproportionate number of these have major marriage problems. Because the original attraction is based on transference, there is a premium on not seeing the prospective partner realistically—especially those aspects of the person that are not like those of the parent. And there is little ability to see the costs of joining someone who frustrates in exactly the same way mother or father frustrated. The possibility of nasty marital surprises is great.

Yet the temptation of a transference-laden relationship, as it develops in courtship, is intense. When young adults are dating, they will occasionally meet someone who means more than the others they are seeing. That meaning is fueled by an opposite-sex person offering the same reward that was craved but not received often enough from the dominant parent. It is further stimulated if the new prospect obviously won't offer the same punishments the parent did. A person who fills this bill usually connects with one at a deeper level, with more intensity, than anyone else, which often leads to the emotional fusion we call falling in love.

The hope in regard to the loved other takes this form: "I love you because you give me a chance to fulfill the dream I've had of getting excited approval (it could be anything) from a person like Dad (it could be either parent, or in some families, a sibling or grandparent)." In itself that isn't bad, in that it gives individuals a way to try to repair an old wound in a thoroughly natural way. That's why it is only those from the field of eligibles who resemble (or are opposite to) the parent in an emotionally powerful way who are admitted to the inner circle. The boon will count only if it comes from someone who is enough like the transference object.

That is why a strongly transference-prone person will pay more attention to the way a prospective mate fits the early model than to whether that person offers anything objectively advantageous. The more motivated by the transference the person is—which typically means the earlier and more severely the person was wounded as a child—the blinder he or she will be to the objective reality of the candidate, and the more strongly moved by the way the candidate does or does not fit the hole in the psyche that has been carried over from childhood.

The tragedy is that most of us try exactly the same methods with the new partner that we used with the dominant parent. And the methods work about the same as they did before— not very well—and for the same reasons they failed before.

Only now the stakes are higher and the pain mounts as the awareness of not getting what is wanted grows. It can take years for either spouse to realize why the marriage is so painful. For many that realization never comes; for others this discovery can be the most redemptive contribution of a successful marital therapy.

## The Transference Must Be Interpreted

Some couples can talk together effectively and still be locked into transference cycles that make their relationship unpleasant. But that's unusual, since the transference cycles themselves generate communication patterns that hide and confuse the actual emotional exchange. The limited gratification the transference produces works even less well if the partners are aware of it, so they create ways of talking to each other that keep deeper levels of reality out of their awareness. Echoing Satir's modes in *Peoplemaking,* they develop punishing or distracting or overfocused (computing) patterns, all of which conceal what is really going on.

The early stages of counseling with such couples will be similar to those used with less damaged relationships. The problem has to be identified, a history has to be taken, and the communicational confusion has to be cleared away. But unlike other couples, these will not experience great relief and sudden improvement when those things are done. The counselor will notice continuing outbursts of unacceptable behavior, acts that each partner knows the other abhors but repeats anyway. Each spouse will continue to believe or claim that the other is motivated by a wish to do harm and will pay little attention to the other's attempts to explain the behavior (and the other's behavior will often take a lot of explaining, since the transference-drivenness of it can be quite cruel and sadistic). Unlike couples who quickly take over the communication process for themselves when you've worked the bugs out, these people show little awareness of or curiosity about their own behavior. No momentum develops; or if it appears to be developing, somebody picks exactly the affront or obstacle that is required to stop it. You will get the impression at points with these couples that you are hearing a conversation that has been repeated many times before. It will feel scripted, automatic, predictably painful. Yet they persist.

When you recognize one of these cycles, which isn't giving anyone new information and is hurting both clients, it is imperative that it be stopped. If the counseling becomes a place where those scenes are replayed, one or both spouses will quickly decide that it isn't any safer here than at home and will leave the counseling. Or even worse, they may find a role for the counselor in the script, transform their two-person game into a three-person one, and carry it on until one of you (often the counselor) is so scarred by it that new symptoms are generated and the escalation reaches a higher level.

There are several ways to stop this, most of which have been described at length in Chapter 5. The counselor must assert authority, overtly or covertly. Yelling "Stop!" at the top of your lungs is one way. You can start doing something that is obviously absurd and get their attention. You can describe the cycle in detail, label it as destructive, and point out the harm it does, again in detail. You can go back to the communication-clarifying techniques in Chapter 6. You can take over the air time, talk hypnotically around in circles for so long that they can't remember the next barb they were going to hurl. Or you can predict the next stage of the cycle, or even ask one of them to do so: "Let's see, Bill, what does Mary do in this fight after you say what you just said?" Sometimes seeing that each already knows the other's lines makes them feel too foolish to say them.

All these methods are ways of stopping the damage, but none produces any change in and of itself (with the possible exception of showing them that there are some ways of stopping the damage). What produces change is interpretation and the new behavior that interpretation stimulates; and it is to this that we turn our attention.

First a warning. Interpretations require a system of understanding the marital relationship, and the character formations that preceded it, in enough detail that the counselor can fit the events of practically any life to the theory. It also requires sufficient clinical experience at knowing when to interpret and how to recognize when an interpretation has been successful, so that the interpretations fit smoothly into the whole therapeutic process. Furthermore, at this level of therapeutic depth, the counselor's own personality problems are more likely to become a factor in the effectiveness of the counseling.

Consequently, I would recommend that the minister who wants to learn and do interpretation-based marriage counseling first do two things: (1) Get enough personal therapy to insure that you will not be a danger to clients, which also will almost always improve your own level of happiness; and (2) find a supervisor or a training program, preferably one accredited by the American Association of Pastoral Counselors, to help you read between the lines of this and other books and apply those learnings to the marital therapy experience with precision and subtlety.

An interpretation is a complex statement or set of statements which links a series of events as cause and effect, joining things the clients had not previously seen as connected, and often including elements that were previously beyond their consciousness. A complete interpretation includes several elements and may be given in pieces, even spanning several sessions, though the counselor is aiming for the ability to combine them in one climactic statement of the whole. The counselor will typically begin with the factors that are most obvious and present, and therefore likely to arouse the least objection from the couple and to produce the least anxiety; and will continue to deepen and extend the interpretation as far as the connections are visible, until the clients' anxiety approaches the limits of tolerability, or the complexity of the interpretation approaches the limits of their ability to follow it.

At least the following elements are part of a complete interpretation: (1) the current difficulty or symptom; (2) the situational crisis out of which the symptom grew; (3) the related failure of the contract, or dream, and the older defensive structure of which the dream has become a piece;

(4) the original childhood purpose of that defense; and (5) the original pain the defense was constructed to protect against.

So a typical interpretation in marital therapy might sound like this: "Joe, when Sally screamed at you (1) and ran back to the bedroom in the middle of your telling her (2) about wanting to change jobs, it seemed to you that she was letting you down, refusing to provide the support (3) she had always provided for you before. That really broke something for you, because Sally doesn't usually act like your mother; and you have always tried to stay away from people like your mom (4) because they exposed you to your own self-doubt and fear (5). Sally is usually a lot more like your dad, much more dependable and less scary."

The immediate purpose of the interpretation is usually to provide both spouses with a more acceptable or less confusing explanation for someone's feelings and behavior than the one they have been using. In Joe's case, the interpretation is an attempt to scale down his feelings by linking them to an old situation that has left him with a reservoir of fear and anger; and by saying it in Sally's presence, you are giving her a way to understand the magnitude of his response, to know why it's important to avoid giving that stimulus and, it is to be hoped, making it unnecessary for her to retaliate.

In the ideal situation, within the same hour, there would be a corresponding interpretation of Sally's actions as well. It might go like this: "Sally, when Joe said he was thinking about quitting his job, it really blew you away (1), and you reacted like you often do when something surprises and frightens you. You knew he was dissatisfied there, but you also know there's a baby coming and there's not much money in the bank (2). You have always valued Joe's solid dependability (3), and it looked for a minute as if he were about to throw you into the same situation your mom was in, when your dad would lose a job and the whole family would be uprooted (4). I think you got a whiff of the terror your family felt when you were six, seven, and eight (5)."

The attempt is to make the reasons for the disturbing behavior obvious and, while thus normalizing the behavior, to illuminate choice-points the couple may not have seen. By pointing out the reasons, you are providing a basis for the elimination of the harsh judgments people often make when someone is hurt. By helping locate choice-points, you make it unnecessary to repeat the behavior.

The interpretation often demonstrates that a piece of the dream was based on an illusion—typically a transference-based illusion—and that the present disruption is happening because they can no longer maintain the illusion. Some aspect of a spouse's reality has broken through the projection, forcing the other to see the spouse as she or he really is and demanding that the other decide how to act in relation to that person as a real person, rather than as a transference object. "He's not your father, he's John," is often the basic intent of the interpretation, followed by, "and you must decide whether you can relate to him as the real person he is, rather than to the image you brought from childhood and attached to him."

An interpretation is needed when a spouse makes the assumption that when the other does something hurtful, the hurt was intended. An important task for an interpretation is to demonstrate that there was a logical reason for what the other did, that it was not done to hurt anyone. If the statement is sufficiently powerful, complete, and precise, both the actor and the spouse will see that there was no way he or she could have done otherwise, given the feelings and information available. But the interpretation should also, if it's complete enough, give both parties enough new information to enable a different action the next time the situation comes up. The counselor is saying at least two things in the same intervention: (1) "Knowing what you knew then, there's nothing else you could have thought or done, and here's why"; and (2) "Now that you know *why* that's true, you no longer need to assume that your former perspective is the only possible one. A broader one is possible, and that enables a different action."

When making the interpretation, the counselor takes an action that had seemed like a solid block, a single undifferentiated event, and breaks it into segments, much like the instant replay of a complicated football play. As the clients see the different steps, perhaps all happening in a few seconds, they also see connections and transitions at which the flow could have been interrupted. For instance, when Joe feels as he did when his mother went screaming out of the room, he has the choice of deciding whether Sally is trying to produce the same feeling his mother did, or that she isn't. If he can see some different reason that Sally is acting that way, it will enable him to have feelings different from those he had toward his mother. Then he has the choice of whether to play it out transferentially, repeating the perception he had of his mother and the feelings it produced, and acting the same way he did, or wanted to, toward his mother; or to decide that those feelings are trying to convince him of a lie—that Sally is identical to his mother—and that he needs to look again and explore whether there are other possible reasons for Sally's behavior. If he makes that choice, he is likely to find those reasons, and then feel the freedom to act differently himself.

In the process of expanding the spouses' information about something that happened between them—a typical consequence of an effective interpretation—two important subjective changes occur. As the counselor sketches out a sequence that includes (and sometimes obviously elicits) evidence of a partner's pain, the other is invited away from preoccupation with his or her own hurt or angry feelings into an awareness of the partner's inner state. Empathy is promoted. At the same time, the interpretation often alerts one or both to a greater complexity in their own motivation than they had realized. Many people find that exciting, arousing their curiosity in a way that directs attention and energy inward, reducing the tendency to blame all pain on the partner. If people can see for the first time how behavioral quirks of their own, previously unnoticed, cause themselves pain by provoking conflict with a spouse, it often motivates them to look further inside and locate other costly facets of their own characters.

Another important contribution of a good interpretation is that it gives both spouses someone different to fight with. A good time for an interpretation is in the early stages of a fight, when the counselor has figured out what the fight is really about. Then the intervention can force them to focus on it rather than on their anger toward each other. If they object to what you say, and they often will, especially if it's right, it allows them to join each other in their opposition to you. This opposition rarely lasts long, but the joining can be an important interruption of their hostility and is often a more important outcome than whatever wisdom the interpretation imparts.

There are some important principles about the timing and frequency of interpretations. Timing is crucial. The right time to interpret is as late as possible. To put it differently, interpret when the partners have given you enough information so that you are sure you have something accurate and valuable to say, but not before the couple has come to the end of productive conversation. If they are talking well together, producing new information for each other, moving toward the solution of some issue, do not interrupt. The only exception to this is very near the end of a session, when you're going to have to interrupt anyway. Ideally, interpretations should be used when their unaided conversation has gone awry, when a fight is brewing, when they have hit an impasse and don't know what to say next, or when the next step in their discussion requires new data that the interpretation will provide. That usually happens late in a session—at least halfway through—since it usually takes that long for them to give you enough new information to have anything to interpret. The purpose of the counseling is to create opportunities for them to talk fruitfully with each other, and the interpretation should serve that by removing obstacles and advancing the conversation. If they are not in trouble in the conversation, and there is still time left in the hour, don't get in their way.

Interpretations should be fairly infrequent, though they should be pivotal when offered. Even in a counseling deliberately centered around interpretation, most of the time is spent preparing to offer one, not actually doing so. One complete major interpretation is quite enough for one session, and many sessions may pass without any at all. There should be, in any session, a small number of partial linkages which might later become a major interpretation, but most of the counselor's time should be spent listening, questioning, blocking disruptive acts, clarifying, and thinking—so that when you have constructed a meaningful set of connections, the clients are ready to hear something from you and have not already had to ward off a flow of words.

Once you have made an interpretation, it is very important to spend the next several minutes—sometimes the next several sessions—assessing its accuracy and usefulness. If you get indications that it hit home, you can add its content to what you know about the couple; if the signals say you missed it, those ideas need to be discarded.

There are three major indicators that an interpretation is accurate and timely. The first is an immediate change in the emotional state of one or both clients, preferably a calming or an intensification, moving in a direction different from the one in which the conversation was headed before you started talking. If you hit it right, they will often feel freed to emote more directly, if they have been ruminating or struggling with a scripted, cyclical conversation; or to drop a trumped-up, politicized emotion and respond from somewhere closer to the center of themselves.

A second clear indicator that you're on the money is the sudden emergence of memories they had not been aware of before (at least recently), or the spontaneous generating of new symbols or images for their situation. The crucial variable here is the spontaneity of the response. If they appear to be surprised by what just came to mind, especially if it carries a rush of feeling, it almost always represents valid confirmation. On the other hand, if they seem to be laboring to say something just to please you, to be good clients, that usually indicates that you have missed the mark—no matter what the content of their words.

The third indicator is visible behavior change, either right then or between sessions. If your interpretation has illuminated the meaning of a specific piece of behavior, and that behavior disappears or changes, you were probably right. If a solution to a problem related to the interpretation comes to the mind of one of them right then or after the session, and it is tried out, that usually means you were right. If their behavior stays about the same, you need to be skeptical about either the content or manner of your intervention.

A major warning: You cannot take their agreement as a mark that you were right. Many people use statements of agreement, especially with people they don't actually agree with, as a major means of resistance and defense. A soft anger turneth away much wrath, and so does an agreement with what seems to be someone's pet idea. Neither can you take disagreement as a definite sign you were wrong. By their fruits you shall know them, and the fruits that need most attention are behavior change, new memories, and alterations in affect.

Successful counseling with more difficult couples will consist of a rhythmic mix of questions, communication clarifiers, confrontations of resistance, and interpretations—with one climactic interpretation every two to five hours. If your interpretations are well chosen, each one that is confirmed will initiate a new cycle of exploration, deepening the level of conversation in a particular area. As the partners explore the region of their relationship that the interpretation invites them into, there will ideally be a rush of excitement at the new discoveries, some sharing with each other about what they mean, and a widening of their sense of mastery and harmony. During that period the counselor's activity can focus largely on communication variables, helping them mine as much out of that exploration as they can get. After a time, often two or three sessions, the momentum from those discoveries will slow down, new resistance will emerge from an as-yet-unresolved area of the relationship. The counselor, gradually sensing the need for an interpretation of the new difficulty, then gathers the data, listening carefully for the deeper meaning of their statements until ready to put words on what is being perceived, and risks the next interpretation.

In an involved marriage counseling case there may be a dozen or more such cycles, and the total work may last a year or more. But sooner or later, in the calm following some particularly pivotal interpretation, either you or one of the spouses will sense that their confidence about mastering their problems has greatly increased. They will notice that the frequency of serious unpleasantness has decreased markedly, and that the regularity with which they solve it—when it does come up—has grown. That signals the approach of the end of your work, and the time to turn serious attention to termination.

# CHAPTER TEN

# $E$NDINGS:
## CELEBRATIONS,
## GRADUATIONS,
## AND REFERRALS

$W$hen the counseling has done its work, the only faithful move is termination. Skillful handling of the ending solidifies the gains your clients have made, sets the stage for further growth, and alerts them to possible pitfalls. It can make the difference between their seeking help if they need it again and deciding that they shouldn't put out the effort—either giving up on the relationship or choosing to suffer in silence.

Referral—the exercise of pastoral care by sending your clients to someone more appropriate for their needs—is an equally difficult and strategic process. There are times when the most caring and skillful counselor is asked for help by someone he or she can't help, at least not right then. Helping that person or couple get into the care of the right person, and helping them get there ready to receive the help they need requires deftness and gentleness, as well as good judgment about both the practitioner receiving the referral and the fit between that person and your people.

In this chapter we will examine each kind of situation, exploring how to assess readiness for termination, how to deal with and avoid premature termination, and how to achieve as much growth as possible during the final phase of the counseling. We will also look at how to decide when a couple should be referred and how to do it with the maximum chance for success.

## The Ending Can Come at Any Point

Though most couple counseling should last at least a few sessions, and most of it much longer, the counselor needs to be thinking about termination from the beginning. Some clients are obviously inappropriate for the counselor to see, and the sooner that is recognized and they are referred, the better. Others will be giving signs from the first minute that they are not likely to stay around long, and the counselor needs to be alert for chances to avoid the termination. And even for couples who are appropriate and pose no threat of terminating too soon, the counselor needs to be clear very soon about what can be achieved before termination, and therefore what criteria for termination the three of you will be aiming for. Often a question like, "How will we know when we're through?" asked in the first session, provides clear signposts for termination and an important reminder to the couple that the counseling relationship is a temporary one, with a specific goal.

### Ending as Soon as You Have Begun

Sometimes you will know in the first ten minutes with clients that you are not the person to help them. When you have thought that through, it is important to overcome the inevitable wish to honor their claim on you. If you are not the best person to do the work, they won't be well served by your attempting it out of guilt.

The most obvious situations for an immediate referral are those in which you have a close personal relationship with one or both partners and have a stronger motivation to enjoy the friendship than to assume the special role of counselor. Most professional therapists will not work with friends, and there are good reasons for pastors to limit work with their personal inner circle to pastoral support and referral. Friends are a lot harder to find than counselees or counselors. Honor that relationship by sending them to someone they can see without interfering with your dinners out or monthly bridge games.

Beyond the complications caused by trying to do counseling with close friends, there are other times when you should not continue. If the person is quite similar to someone with whom you have a relationship that is not resolved, it is dangerous to do counseling with them. The feelings about that other relationship are too likely to become involved in this one.

It is awkward at best, and often dangerous, to attempt counseling with a key leader in your congregation. If your board chairman comes to you with a marital problem, immediately explore that person's willingness to accept referral. Other parishioners will need you more as a public figure, a leader in worship or community; you may sense that becoming their counselor would leave them without a priest or preacher.

Or you may discover in the first hour that the personal pathology of a couple is greater than you are trained to handle, or is of a variety that you, trained or not, find unpleasant to work with.

These are perfectly valid reasons for declining an invitation to counsel. There is another crucial reason: You may not have the time. The more deeply pained the clients, the more time they will take, especially in the early sessions. The more complicated the role involvements, the more time they will take, and the more they will complicate your other professional responsibilities. The closer they are to the growing edge of your own learning, the more you will want to think and read about the problems they present. Seeing clients they don't have time to see or ought to turn away for other reasons often leaves counselors resenting the visits, angry at the clients for needing help, and less available to them and to the rest of his or her responsiblities. Though it is tempting to try to be all things to all people, beyond a certain point, everyone is damaged by the attempt. Set a limit on how many hours you want to spend counseling, and when you reach it, avoid further commitments. Saying yes once can commit dozens of hours over the course of months.

When you do discover, for whatever reason, that a couple is not one you should continue with, it's important to act promptly on that decision. Clients invest a lot of hope in their counselors, and the more attached they get to you, the harder it will be to refer them without damage. Literally, every minute you wait makes it harder for the eventual referral to take hold. Make a clear statement at a natural break in the flow of conversation. Tell them you cannot continue with them, give them as much of the reason as is useful, and offer immediately to put them in touch with someone who can help: "I'm awfully pleased you've decided to work on this problem. It's obviously caused a lot of pain. Unfortunately, I'm not the person best suited to work with you. I leave in three days for a month's vacation, and your difficulty needs attention long before I would be in a position to provide it. But I do know an excellent marriage counselor who specializes in difficulties like yours, and her office is within a few blocks. I'd like to give you her name and number, and perhaps give her a call to let her know to expect a word from you. How would that be with you?"

The referral process will be discussed further later in the chapter.

### Moving Them on After the Air Is Clear

There are occasions when it is not an option to refer clients immediately, but it is equally unwise to continue beyond the crisis phase. This usually happens when they have come to you in an emergency, with an unmistakable expectation that you are the one to help them.

If your sister calls from the next town and urgently sobs that her husband is sitting in the bedroom with a gun to his head, you don't stop and argue about the proper person to give the help. You get to the next town as fast as you can, knowing that what must be done now is to get the gun out of his hand. In the process, you make a commitment to stay with them until the suicide risk has calmed. Once they accept that there is hope if specific obstacles can be removed, you can refer them to someone better placed to help get rid of the obstacles.

Pastors and other frontline professionals are often in this position. A call may come from people who are closer to you than would be comfortable for long-term work, but their trust provides you with the necessary authority to shepherd them through an emergency. During the acute upheaval, your closeness and history together is an asset. There are a lot of questions you don't need to ask, and they have already tested you out—they know you can help.

That is a time for fast, directive, problem-focused work. You want to find out what has happened, what the causal links are, and what options they have tried and are considering. Once that is accomplished, your task is to provide them a time perspective, giving them relief from the urgent fear that the pain must stop right now or it will destroy them. In such situations people usually narrow their focus, so they miss possible options. They often exaggerate the dangers of delay and believe that circumstances won't permit time to think. You can help them find ways of slowing things down so they can consider the alternatives you can provide and quiet the inner voices that are demanding immediate action.

If you help them restore a sense of safety, relieving the immediate danger of suicide, violence, divorce, flight, or hospitalization, you have often re-created their sense of being in charge of their destiny. Once that is reestablished, together, you can plan a more orderly approach to the concerns that were so frightening. Once they see that there may be a way out, the panic diminishes and the focus shifts to accomplishing the things that must be done. This both increases hope and begins the process of problem solving that will be the substance of whatever counseling they seek.

Pastors often know at once that a crisis is theirs to ride out, but that the total work will be more than they should do. When you know that, it is important to begin thinking immediately about what must be accomplished before you can safely remove yourself. It's even good to say, once things have begun to ease up, "I think I should see you every day until Mary gets back to town (or John gets out of the hospital, or Sam calls AA), and then we'll see about getting you together with a specialist in problems like this."

Another situation is ideal for referral—when you sense that the couple has defeated you. That can happen early or late, but your move to refer should be immediate when you realize you have made a major error and no recovery is possible (as in the case of sexual seduction, or violence); or when you realize that this couple is of a type you never do well with. That recognition may come later if the counseling is going around in repeated cycles that leave you confused and frustrated. No counselor can successfully treat every couple, and admitting failure early is less expensive to all concerned than admitting it late. That should always be done in a discussion that provides clients a thorough opportunity to express whether they think they are getting what they need—and their response does need to be heard—but unless they are getting something you were not aware of, you need to move them on: "I've noticed that the last four or five times you've been in, we've been saying the same things to each other, and it doesn't seem that much is changing at home. I think that's because you need someone with more experience in situations like yours, and possibly with more time to devote to it. I'd like to help you find such a person to work with, and I can go back to being your pastor and friend."

### Quitting Because You Have Succeeded

The endings we all prefer are the celebrations. The three of you have defined the problem, clarified the contract, cleaned up the communication, and interpreted when necessary. The improvement is obvious. The clients talk to each other more often and more successfully. They report fewer and less serious eruptions of the conflicts that brought them in. They are less needy for sessions. They report that even when their fights or other problems do get started, they're able to stop them with minimal damage. In the sessions, they obviously are enjoying each other more, and your interventions are required less often. Their focus has shifted away from blaming toward self-understanding and self-curiosity. Finally, they either begin missing sessions or are less impatient to schedule them and begin talking about when to end the counseling.

## A Clean Ending Seals the Gains

A clear and mutually satisfying termination is an accomplishment for both couple and counselor. It helps secure whatever progress has been made by demonstrating for the clients that they can handle a difficult human transaction in a satisfying way. When everybody knows that the counseling is over, when and why it ended, what was accomplished, and what is left to do, it marks a clear punctuation point, the end of a troubled piece of life and the opening of a new period, with acknowledged different possibilities.

Whenever possible, end by mutual agreement. Your confirmation of the clients' readiness adds to the readiness, and your judgment of unreadiness (if applicable) is an important part of the professional opinion for which they sought you out.

### Knowing When to Stop

*They may tell you.*

Often clients will state directly that they think it is time to stop. If this is said when they have had an obvious success or conquered a known obstacle, leaving the path before them clear, the only appropriate thing for you is to agree. If you do, say so and begin to plan for a date. Usually that will not be at the end of the immediate session, though sometimes that is acceptable. More often you will need at least one more session to review the work that has been done and focus on saying your good-byes. A useful rule of thumb is to allow between 5 and 10 percent of the total counseling time for the process of terminating. People get into trouble from ending relationships badly as often as they do by beginning them badly; your termination needs to help them end this one well and learn from that experience.

If they say they are ready but you are uncertain, ask them to say more. Listen for their report of successes. Don't express an opinion immediately, but suggest instead that the three of you explore their readiness. Ask them to tell you about the things that have led them to consider ending the sessions, the criteria they are using to decide that the time is near.

In situations in which the wisdom of terminating is unclear to you, it is important not to undercut the couple's confidence. If the clients seem definite, and you don't have a strong opinion either way, accept a "let's stop for now and see how it goes" decision. That will give them the advantage of experiencing your trust in their competence and avoid the occasionally unpleasant feelings that come from escaping counseling against the counselor's dogged opposition. That, in turn, makes it easier for them to come back later if they need to.

On the other hand, if you have strong misgivings about their terminating, those feelings should alert you to look more closely at their intentions. If there are particular areas you don't believe are resolved, ask about them. Listen carefully to their response, and if they say things that are not completely clear, pursue the answers until they are fully clarified. If the questionable areas are still questionable, and if your questions and their answers don't remove your misgivings, state them clearly but undemandingly: "I'm concerned. It seems nothing has changed in your pain over the way your wife is with her mother. If that is still capable of producing as much conflict as it used to, it could really throw you the next time she comes for a visit."

By making your doubts specific, you challenge them to present their best case for readiness, and it is doubly important that you listen carefully to their response and assess the strength of what they say. Often they will have developed confidence and competence you had not noticed and will reveal it now. If they do, the change needs to be acknowledged and weighed. On the other hand, if they don't convince you that your misgivings are in error, you need to do two things: (1) Let them know you still have doubts, though you recognize that they remain in charge of the decision; and (2) see if you can ascertain any other, irrational, reasons for their wanting to terminate at this particular time.

A move to terminate that is not backed up by solid improvement must come from some other motivation. That, in turn, can be sought among three possible sources: counselor error that has offended or frightened them; fear that comes from the healthy movement of the process; and external pressure. You can often ascertain which it is by asking them to trace the history of their thinking about termination. If it began to occur the night after you had forgotten their appointment, or been late, or called them by the wrong names, you can suspect that the idea began in their anger about your breach of the relationship. More subtle errors can produce the same results: a mistaken interpretation which they find offensive or the counselor's insistence on a time change for the sessions. When they tell you directly that you did something that damaged their faith in the relationship, or when the history of their thinking about termination leads you to that conclusion, you are in a position to acknowledge your error, correct any effects that are correctable, and commit yourself to not repeating it. This often restores their faith in your good will and believability, allowing the counseling to get back on track.

On the other hand, an attempt to flee may develop out of the fear produced by accelerated growth. Growth always puts people in new situations, and they don't know exactly how to behave. They may experience an upsurge in sexual desire or anger, or have impulses to try new things, simply because of their feeling that life is less inhibited. That in turn may stretch their ability to control their actions, and they may be frightened of going crazy or behaving irresponsibly. Not being sure they can keep control of their lives, and identifying the counseling as the cause of the upset, they may consider ending it. This kind of termination threat can usually be managed with reminders that they have not actually done anything dangerous and that part of maturity is the ability to feel one's whole range of feelings and still decide for responsible behavior. You can point out that maintaining those decisions in the face of stronger impulses is like developing muscles in any physical task: the more difficult the task, the stronger the muscles will grow. But one does not expect to pick up a three-hundred-pound object in the first attempt at body-building. One works up to it.

The other occasional source of an otherwise inexplicable termination threat is external pressure. The husband's mother may run into an unaccustomed burst of his anger and mutter something guilt-producing about the effects of counseling. An employer may learn of the counseling and view it as a symbol of mental instability. The wife's lover may tell her that there isn't anything wrong with her life that he can't solve and make her willingness to end the counseling a condition for maintaining their relationship. Sometimes these external pressures remain hidden, like the wife's lover; and sometimes they are not alterable, like the husband's boss (I was told by one client that it is the policy of a company in our area to fire any management employee who seeks counseling). But most external pressures can be managed, and their management can be a part of the clients' growth. Clarifying the nature of the pressure opens the possibility of helping plan ways to meet it and, if necessary, practicing the skills the clients will need to challenge its sources.

Sometimes, even when your misgivings are strong and unanswered, a client couple will persist in the intent to terminate. If you see that this intent is unchangeable, it is important to yield in a way that keeps the door open. If you become angry, defensive, insulting, or accusing, it will be harder for the clients to return if things go badly. Better to acknowledge their right to control that decision, remind them that you don't believe the work is finished, alert them to probable danger points in the near future, and invite them to return if they need you. A response like this may do it: "I can see that you believe it's time to end our sessions. You know I'm concerned about the risks when the baby's born and would like to see your margin of safety a little broader. But this does need to be your decision, and I respect the attempt you're making. If things do get harder in a few weeks, you know where to find me."

This is a good time to tell them whether you expect any changes that would limit their access. If you expect to be changing parishes in six months, it would be good to let them know: "In case it would make a difference in your coming again, you should know that I expect to be here only until May." Often that will help them return in March if they need to, rather than letting things drag out until they can't possibly wait any longer.

*You may tell them.*

Many times couples will reveal signs that the work is finished, without telling you directly that they are ready to quit. This can stem from politeness, their deference to your authority, or from their not having realized that their increasing sense of well-being had reached the point where they should trust it.

There are several indicators to alert you that it is time to mention termination. The clients may arrive for three or four consecutive sessions with nothing to work on, feeling fairly good. You will ask some questions to find whether there are areas of pain they are hiding, and you won't find any. They will tell you about situations wherein they are mastering difficulties they could not handle earlier, situations that previously would have triggered the problems that brought them into counseling. They will begin to talk about a time after the counseling is completed, how they're going to use the spare time and, if applicable, money. Or they may mention in passing that it is getting more difficult to free time for the sessions, or that the cost, if any, is beginning to pinch (a fee that seemed modest in an emergency will begin to feel much more expensive when clients are comfortable).

If you have noticed signs like these, and listening for a few minutes does not produce anything that contradicts them, then it's up to you to raise the termination question: "It sounds as though you have accomplished most of what you came for" or "I think you're telling me that you're ready to end these sessions." If you don't get any objection, move into the same pattern you would have used if they had initiated the conversation. Usually that will involve setting a termination date and planning toward it, though occasionally your asking about their readiness will stimulate them to bring up that one remaining issue they had been putting off till later. Some couples will go through two or three such almost-terminations before they finish everything they need to settle.

### Mark the Ending Clearly

It's important for both counselor and clients to know exactly when the counseling is finished. You do not need the uncertainty that comes from not knowing whether this couple still has a claim on your time, and the clients also suffer an uneasiness if they merely drift away from the process. Part of the loss is that the lack of a closing session deprives all parties of the chance to finish the process, as we will be discussing below. But beyond that, it teaches something about the way agreements function to have a point where everybody knows that their responsibilities to one another are, for the time being, completed.

A clear ending is a bit harder to achieve with couples than when counseling individuals. Usually with individuals there is enough dependency on the counselor that the parting is a wrenching experience. Nobody can ignore it. But in marital counseling the dependency is invested more in the partner, so that the counselor never becomes as personally important, and therefore is easier to leave. But drifting away doesn't serve anyone well. If a session ends without a clear statement that there will or won't be another, get it clarified. Call or write. The same holds if the clients have cancelled a session and not made it clear whether they want another. Your contact needs to make it clear that it is acceptable for them not to return—if it is—but that you need to know whether to continue to hold time for them. On the other hand, if you are pretty sure these folks need to continue the process, part of your professional responsibility is to say so. You don't have subpoena power, but they have a right to expect a warning from you if you see them racing toward a precipice.

Though it is important to get clear closure, it is also important to avoid begging people to come for help they don't want. If a couple leaves an ending ambiguous, but I am convinced they don't plan to return, I will convey that in my contact: "Your cancellation a month ago, and my not having heard from you since, leave me assuming that you don't plan to continue our work. Since I need to make other plans for the time we were using, I'll close your file and free that time for other counselees if I haven't heard something from you by the first of next week (January 3). I wish you well in your search for continued growth in your marriage." A month is really too long to wait before following up on a cancellation, unless you don't want to see the people again or know they were at an appropriate point for termination anyway. But this kind of call is an easy one to forget, especially if your counseling load is so full that you don't relish an additional hour.

Another situation to avoid zealously is calling counselees several times to find out whether they want to schedule another appointment, having them say yes and then either cancelling it or not showing up. Some people have a very difficult time saying they don't want to see you any more. After one such cancellation or no-show, if I choose to call them again (rather than write), I will say that the cancellation sounds like a message about wanting to quit and ask them to tell me if that's the case. Then if I object, I can say why and ask them to come in and let me say it in person. If their quitting doesn't seem like a problem, I can either make that official on the phone or schedule one more hour for the purpose of saying goodbye and wrapping up the loose ends.

### Assessing and Grieving

The final session of any counseling should include a free-flowing assessment of the progress that has been made, and a request for feedback from the clients about what was and was not helpful. If you have notes from the first session, it can be helpful to read what they wanted from the counseling at that point. Then you and they can decide how much of it they got, and what the most important factors were in their getting it, and in not getting more. If things have gone well, clients usually receive more than and something different from what they came in asking for. They will usually have removed some obvious symptoms, but will also have discovered some abilities and had some experiences together they would not have known how to ask for at the beginning.

If the outcome is a happy one, a little dreaming about the future can help you end on a high note. "What do you see as the next major steps for the two of you?" can get that conversation going. It also serves to get their energy out of the counseling and into their own future, which is where it belongs.

If the counseling has not been able to accomplish all it set out to do, the dreaming needs to be different. To whatever extent the effort has been a failure, they need to decide on the implications of the failure. Does it mean divorce? or referral? or individual therapy? or making do with a less wide-ranging or enjoyable relationship than had been hoped? It's important not to leave these questions floating in their minds, with each wondering what the other is thinking. You are in a position to convert that uncertainty into definite planning: "I know we haven't accomplished all you had hoped. Have you decided what that means to your relationship and how you need to proceed?"

Whether the work has gone well or badly, there are going to be feelings about its ending. People will usually be sad about leaving the specialness of the counseling relationship, even if they continue to see you in other capacities. They need a chance to tell you that, to say something of what it's meant to them to work with you. That's especially important if the feelings are not altogether positive, and in most cases there is a mixture of feelings. People often are ashamed of needing help in the first place, and that clouds their satisfaction with it when it is good. And the counselor may have made some mistakes or challenged some favorite assumptions, leaving anger in the clients as a result. They need a chance to say what they have been angry about, as well as what they have appreciated. (Note: This is different from their assessment of what you did well or badly. They might have been, and still may be angry about some of your moves, even though they know they helped them.) They need to tell you about their relief that the counseling is finished, as well as their sadness that they are losing the specialness with you.

There are two important reasons that these emotions be made explicit. The more of this they can put into words, the less the relationship will feel unfinished, and the more energy they will have to take into the future. But it is also an important piece of modeling. If they can see you dealing with their positive and negative emotions about the relationship, they can learn something about handling endings with other people, and about nondefensively asking for and receiving feelings of both kinds from each other.

Of course, the counselor has feelings about the ending of the work as well, and it can be redemptive to share them. Most people who come for counseling have some doubts about whether anyone wants to invest much in them. If being part of their lives has been meaningful to you, it can be part of their healing to hear this. Your sadness at their leaving, if it exists, is also a gift to them; and sharing it can help you let go of the relationship. After this session you and they go back to being peers, co-citizens of the community and participants in whatever shared efforts exist, and it's important for the feelings that have been developed in the counseling to be contained, shared, and resolved there.

### The Last Look Forward

In the last few minutes of counseling, I like to review whatever likely pitfalls any of us can think of that might take place during the next few weeks or months. By doing so I'm trying to seal the success of the work we have accomplished and establish a watchfulness about this couple's specific vulnerabilites. I might ask, "If you were going to get into trouble again, how would it probably happen?" or "What danger signals should you look for to let you know it's time to come back?" or "What are the dangers for your marriage that you see in the next several months?" It is important to establish for them, preferably from their own words, the realistic points of remaining weakness or vulnerability. Once that's done, you can say, "If that does come up again, how do you hope to handle it?" You are trying to establish an agreed-upon set of tactics for managing a type of difficulty they know they are adept at creating, though you all hope they're less inclined to create it than before.

Once that is in place, you can close with the combination of an acknowledgment that none of us is ever perfect, so you can't say for sure that these troubles will not come up again, and whatever assurance you can offer them about their probable future success: "We can't fully predict the future, but I'm confident that the skills we've worked on will keep you from ever getting back to where you were last March, if you're consistent in using them."

Then all that's left is to say good-bye, leaving the door open in a way that is both a genuine invitation and an expression of confidence that they won't need it: "It's been a joy to work with you. I'd love to see you again, but I hope and trust it will be under happier circumstances. If you do need me, you know where to call."

Firm handshakes, hugs, invitations to send a Christmas card or a baby announcement are fully appropriate here. It is important that when they leave the office this time, they know that your relationship is permanently different, that you have returned to your roles as pastor and parishioner, or citizens in the same city, or fans of the same football team. Your special claim on each other has ended, though there remains the warmth of everyone's memories and the implicit promise that if such work should be needed again, you would be available to do it (if that's true—if it is not, because of some change in your situation, they need to know that). I always assure my terminating clients that they have first claim on my time if they should need me again, but that I hope their lives go so well that they can't find time to see me.

### Referral: A Loving Pastoral Act

Many times you are not the best person to help a couple. As has been discussed, there are numerous reasons that might require passing a couple on to another professional better situated to provide the necessary care. But pastors often assume that their responsibility ends with the decision to refer, missing the important difference between a good referral and a bad one. Making a referral that works is a delicate and difficult process, and requires as much care and concentration as the counseling itself.

### *Your Authority Goes with Them*

Couples seek you out because you have gained their trust, either directly through an ongoing relationship, or on the strength of someone else's word. If you handle their referrals properly, that authority and trust will accompany them to the person you name as the probable source of help. This is utterly crucial, because research makes unmistakably clear that an expectation of getting help is the most important factor in actually getting it. If you can handle a transition so couples arrive at the receiving person expecting help as fully as when they arrived in your office, you have helped them greatly.

An important step in that transition is making it clear to clients why you are referring them. If your reasons are good ones, your care for them will be obvious; and the respect for their feelings demonstrated by explaining what might seem like a rejection is not lost on them. The intent here is to provide enough information so they will know, later, if not immediately, that your choice not to continue is the most caring thing you could do, the thing that most took their needs into account. Those reasons can include the expertise of the person to whom you are referring, which you can detail; the factors that limit your own availability, such as an overfull schedule, or church policy, or a pending move or vacation; limitations on your competence in situations like theirs; or factors in your relationship with them that make counseling its least fruitful expression. This explanation needs to be given whether requested or not, and it needs to be given nondefensively and with sensitivity for their feelings: "I've decided that it is not wise for me to continue working on these problems with you. As you know, the church's capital fund drive begins in three weeks, and my heavy involvement there means my time will be quite dear, and you need someone who is more available. There is a new pastoral counselor in the community, who still has room in her caseload and has published two papers on problems identical to yours. I think you should see her."

Once you have made a firm and clear statement of your unavailability, followed by your explanation of the reasons, you need to hear the clients' feelings about both the referral and the reasons. If they don't volunteer any, ask for them. This is crucial, because people almost always feel disappointed and angry about being referred. It is a rejection. Those feelings need to stay in the relationship with you, and the only way for that to happen is for you to invite their expression. If they remain unexpressed, they will be aimed at the new counselor and stand as a barrier. You do that person a real favor, not to mention improving your parishioners' prospects in the counseling, to make sure those feelings are directed at yourself. And once directed, they need a response. Again, defensiveness will damage the referral, so you need to accept the reality and appropriateness of their disappointment, while at the same time hoping they can understand the factors that led to your decision: "It was an honor to have you ask me for help, and a disappointment to me that it doesn't work out for us together. Given the confidence we have developed in each other, I can understand that it is disappointing to you as well. But the factors I've mentioned are real, and I don't think it would be helpful to you if I ignored them."

If you haven't done so while explaining your reasons for the referral, give them as much information about the person and setting you are referring them to as they want and you have. Especially important are data about the individual's credentials, expertise, and areas of specialization; but it can also be useful to share something of the person's faith perspective, if that is likely to be a positive force for your couple. Once you have passed on the information about the new counselor, be sure to ask if the clients have questions. If they do, answer them if you can and if it seems proper. Your intent should be to help them find things in the new person that sound familiar enough to provide a link, ways that the counselor is like you, since you are the person they sought out originally.

They can also use administrative information about the counselor's situation. If you know how fees are handled, tell them. If you have the phone number or address, give it to them. If there is anything at all complex about the intake procedure in the new office, be sure they know it. If you suspect there is a waiting list, alert them to that. This is also a good time to let them know whether there is a connection between your congregation, or you personally, and the counselor or the center in which the counselor practices. If the person is in a pastoral counseling center, and your congregation contributes money to that center, be sure they know it. It establishes a link across which your authority can move. If the counselor is your friend, say so; if he or she was your therapist, tell them that. It provides more basis for their confidence, which is a powerful healing factor.

Once you have filled in the objective data about the counselor and any personal or administrative links between you, offer to make a contact. "I'd like your permission to call and let him (or her) know to expect to hear from you." Again, that has the effect of your going at least part way to the new counselor's office with them, making the barrier they have to climb a little lower.

Finally, assure them of your continued interest, invite them to keep you posted on their progress, and tell them what kind of feedback you typically get from this counselor. Again, you are trying to make the relationship with the new person somewhat like a subsection of their relationship with you. The more they sense your presence going to the new office with them, the greater the chance that they will arrive confident and ready to work.

### Contacting the Other Counselor

When you have told your couple you will call the person you are referring them to, it is important to do it. If you don't, they always find out, which makes it easier for them to doubt the other things you have said about the referral. But beyond that, the contact helps your couple directly in important ways.

To begin with, it increases their chances of getting in. Most excellent pastoral counselors, or marriage and family therapists, are very busy and must turn away more new clients than they take. As someone who is often in that position, I know that a call from a friend or a person whose referrals I particularly want makes it more likely that I will find room for their referral when that person makes contact. It's easier to turn down someone or refer them to another counselor if their call is unexpected and not backed up by a message from someone I want to please. If you can think of something to say to the receiving counselor that makes it more attractive to see these particular clients, so much the better.

Your call also gives the new counselor a chance to let you know of any problems on that end. If there is a waiting list, or the fees have gone up, the office has moved, or if someone there knows the clients personally, the contact gives them a chance to tell you. Then you can alert the couple or reconsider the referral.

It's also a good idea to let the receiving counselor know anything that would affect scheduling of the clients' appointments, so you can find out if that will pose impossible problems. If your clients both work from eight to five, can never get off to go to the doctor or anywhere else, and the counselor works the same hours and never makes exceptions, it's best for you to find that out before you connect the clients' hopes inextricably with this new person. Anything you can do to increase the clients' success in obtaining counseling decreases the danger that they will give up until their marriage is in more serious trouble.

The call gives you a chance to remind the receiving counselor, and yourself, that you share a mutual ministry with these clients, and to do any fence mending or other planning to enhance that ministry. It also gives you a chance to check out that counselor's attitude toward you and your work and to get an idea about the feedback and cooperation you can expect. It is possible that the new person will be too busy to keep you informed, but the call gives you a chance to negotiate that. The counselor will probably remind you that he or she can't tell you much without the clients' permission, which in turn gives you something to discuss with the clients.

### *Establishing and Celebrating a Mutual Ministry*

One of the vital acts for the frontline professional new to a work setting is the developing of a network of relationships for professional referral. A huge range of persons offer human services, and they cover immense diversities of attitude and expertise. Some are very good, some not-so-good, and some genuinely harmful. The phone-book ads won't tell you who's who, with the possible exception of providing professional credentials—and those are far from being the most important variable. Credentials usually establish only minimal standards, and in some states, not even that.

The only reliable guides to competent and compatible partnership in counseling are your own personal impressions and those of others in your community whom you trust. Take advantage of the continuing education opportunities counselors and their centers offer—more to learn about the counselors than the subject matter. Accept the luncheon invitations new counselors often extend, to get to know whether this is a person you would trust with people you care about. Notice who offers programs for ministerial associations and local churches, and which of them are worth the time (a warning—counselors who are very busy, especially those in private practice, may not need to do workshops and other training events for public relations. Don't assume that their not offering them is necessarily a sign of disinterest or incompetence; rather that they are busy and do not need new cases right now. On the other hand, larger agencies almost always offer training events, busy or not, to keep their name before the public.)

If you think of such luncheons and workshops as work time, aimed toward getting as much data as possible about the usefulness of this resource in your ministry, you can get a lot out of them. Ask what kind of counseling or therapy the people do, what they have written, who trained them, what they charge and why, what excites them about the work they do, and why they are interested in having contact with you. If you get answers that make sense and are compatible with your beliefs and interests, put those people or places higher on your list of potential options than those you have not met.

Another important principle is to refer to *persons* rather than to *centers*, when possible. There are wide variations of experience and interest within the staffs of most centers. Though you can count on a rough similarity of attitude and commitment, that may not tell you much about the personal fit between the counselor and yourself or your people. Counseling is a profoundly personal enterprise, and the more clearly you can imagine the chemistry between a given parishioner and a particular therapist, the more likely your referral is to be helpful.

Once you have made those contacts and gotten that information, the referrals that follow serve as a reminder to the counselor of the shared ministry. Your referrals give you a claim on the one who receives them; and a therapist who wants to be a partner in ministry will also want to honor that claim. Ask that person for information, for consultation, for educational events, and you will usually be rewarded. Ultimately, the greatest reward for both of you comes from the discovery of personal enrichment in fellowship and cooperation with each other, which enhances both ministry and life itself.

Neither ministry nor life is ever an isolated phenomenon. Both flower when stimulated and fertilized by other practitioners, faithfully striving to combine resources for greater effectiveness and to join spirits for fuller understanding. Faith pushes us to continue expanding our knowledge and our vision, and the sharing between professionals who are struggling to bring light out of human darkness can be a profound reward. In that sense, professional collaboration shares much with the intimacy of healthy marriage and the communion of the kingdom of God. In all three, the knowledge, ideas, and energy that emerge in any member strain the boundaries of the individual, longing to reach out and bear fruit in contact with the other, and with God's great mystery.